BIRTHING

OUT OF

MY

WILDERNESS

Suzette A. Fox

DEDICATION

I return this book back to my heavenly Father who has poured into me and entrusted me to scribe His words within this book to propel His people into their purpose and destiny.

~

I dedicate this book to my mentor, Mother Andrea Carn. During my mentorship, Mother Carn saw in me what I never saw in myself—the ability to write books inspired by God. This book began with me daily journaling, which helped me to overcome a very dark place in my life. During my mentoring sessions, Mother would always say to me, "I'm enjoying your book." On the other end of the phone, I would just nod my head in agreement but was not convinced. However, as I continued to journal I began to see the blessing this book would be for someone. I am thankful and grateful for Mother's insight and for her allowing God to use her to bring me out of a very dark place and into birthing this book.

~

I also dedicate this book to my children. Through writing this book, it has transformed me and renewed my mind to be a better God-fearing mother, to lay all my cares aside and to build a healthier relationship with my children.

ACKNOWLEDGMENTS

I thank God for trusting and inspiring me to write His book and for His divine connection to my author coach, Minister Tiffany Jordan, CEO of Tiffany Jordan Ministries. I am also thankful for my editor and to all those behind the scenes praying and imparting their knowledge and skills to bring this empowering book into fruition.

To my parents, Nella and Leroy Franklyn, whom God chose to be my parents to love and care for me and raise me up in the Lord which shaped me to be the woman I am today;

To my spiritual parents, Apostle Darryl Walton and Pastor Dr. Keisha Walton of Emmanuel Apostolic Temple; Pastor Arthur C. Naylor and Barbara Naylor of First Pentecostal Prayer of Faith Church where my spiritual journey started;

And to all the other pastors, first ladies and leaders whom God choose to impart to, nurture and groom me spiritually to be the woman of God I am today, my children and I say

thank you.

CONTENTS

Introduction

YOUR ARMOUR

INTRODUCTION

As I ponder what the children of Israel went through as slaves in Egypt under the rulership of Pharaoh, being overseen by a taskmaster and overwhelmed with a significant amount of work, they experienced minimal freedom and privileges. But they cried to God day and night trusting in Him to one day deliver them. God, our great Provider and Deliverer, had the ultimate plan to deliver His people out of the hands of Pharaoh through Moses and Aaron. Moses was the mouthpiece God used to send messages to Pharaoh, who was persistent in holding God's people in bondage. God had to show him who has all power and authority. With the force of God's hand, Pharaoh had no other choice but to let God's people go, even after pursuing them to the Red Sea.

This story reminds me of my life and how I birthed this book. I was once a slave to the desires of this world which is a representation of Egypt. I was truly a slave to the desires of this world without knowing it. Ancestral prayers released me out of the hands of the enemy the same as the Israelites ancestral prayers broke them free from the bondage of Pharaoh. I fought my way through, it was not easy, but I persisted and kept my head above it and focused on God. For Moses and Aaron, it was not an easy task to face Pharaoh each time God directed them to and deliver the message, "Let My people go." In comparison, in our daily lives, Pharaoh can be compared to Lucifer and Moses and Aaron to our intercessors and prayer warriors who seek God's face to get us out of Egypt and back in fellowship with Him. God used Moses and Aaron to face Pharaoh because He so desired for the Israelites to be free to worship Him.

In Exodus, chapter 14, as the Israelites made their way through the wilderness to the Promised Land, they became fearful because of what was before them and made it known to Moses they were better off in Egypt. I recall that when I experienced my trials, I would say the same, "God, have you forsaken me?" I had this great idea that after being born again, I would not have any more problems in life. Oh, what a misconception that was! Same as the Israelites believed, on their way to the Promised Land, that they will not have any trials, but Moses reminded them that the God of Abraham, Isaac and Jacob would see them through. Exodus 14:13 says, "And Moses said unto the people, Fear ye not, stand still, and see the salvation of the Lord, which he will shew to you to day: for the Egyptians whom ye have seen to day, ye shall see them again no more forever." Just as Moses spoke to the Israelites, He is also talking to us as born-again Christians. While we are running for our lives, here comes our adversary trying to remind us of the so-called "good ol' days" when we were in the world with him. Little do we know that God is using our trial to cleanse and purge us and bring us in alignment with Him to fulfill our purpose on Earth. But thank God for a praying man or woman of God who will whisper in our ear or from the pulpit that God will see us through and to just hold on to God's unchanging hands.

Like the Israelites sojourning through the wilderness to the Promised Land, so was I sojourning in my life through the wilderness to my destiny. The Israelites knew God through Moses and not for themselves, and so did I. I did not know God for myself, but only relied on the man or woman of God who preached the word. As Jethro stated to Moses in Exodus 18:13-22, it was his job to teach the people the laws and ways of God, but not to be their god. At some point, we have to seek for that authentic relationship with God or else we will base our walk with God on religion as some of the Israelites did. They complained about every difficult task they experienced and so did I because I did not know God for myself. I went on this journey for years of being hot and cold for God. I religiously attended practically all scheduled services, prayer meetings and conference after conference. I fasted and went on many times of consecration in my life. I would be on fire for the Lord and next thing you know, here comes "Mr. Trial," and I would melt like butter because I did not know who God truly was. I have made many, many wrong decisions because of not knowing who God is and had to live with the consequences, but in spite of it, I held on to God's hand and he never let me go.

In 2014, my life made a devastating turn which impacted me greatly. I found myself in an even more bewildered place not knowing who I was in God and who

God was in me. I kept pressing my way through, but it was a very rough road. Through it all, God showed Himself to me many times so that my faith would increase in Him. I found myself second guessing God even when I knew He was right there with me to bring me through.

Two years later, in 2016, my life made a turn for the best. God directed me to quit my job at Amazon and drive for Uber and to also return to school. I was very comfortable at Amazon. I had a stable job finally and was able to keep my house, pay my bills on time and care for my children. But God saw the bigger picture that I did not see. I can recall it like it happened yesterday. It was Thursday, September 8, 2016, and I had dreamt that I was at the altar during a women's conference wailing, "God, I surrender my all." I was scheduled to attend the conference on Friday, September 9. That Friday, as I entered into the sanctuary of the conference, the glory of the Lord was very thick in the house. I could not contain myself but just wept like a baby as God ministered to me. After the conference ended, I stayed seated while I listened to His voice. His direction was for me to fast, pray, and consecrate as I meditated and studied the book of Ephesians. I sat in my seat and fought within myself saying, "God, this can't be. I can't take a week off. I have bills to pay and I have NO PTO or SICK DAYS to compensate my time." But God said, "Trust Me." At that time, my idea of trusting in God amounted to me "helping God," by taking control of everything and thinking I was on the correct path of faith. Once I got home, I settled down and did what the Lord told me to do. It was one of the toughest days of my life, not being in control. And that's when my crushing began—when He began birthing me out of my wilderness. This time spent with God was my open heaven allowing me to come into alignment with Him and His purpose for my life. It doesn't end there! At this time, my car was in the shop more than it was on the road, bills were being backed up, and I started contemplating in my mind "I need to apply for unemployment." The Holy Spirit literally held my hand from submitting my application. Then I had the bright idea to call my dad. The Holy Spirit did not allow me even to pick up the phone to call him. Then I decided to continue "helping God" and reached out to my brother. I sent him a message to call me, and when he called me back, I could not utter a word to him as to what I needed. My hands were too short to box God. I settled myself down and took my crushing like a big girl, which proved to be very intense. Many nights I would cry myself to sleep saying, "God, why are you doing this to me?" To help me deal with this "crushing," I recalled God connecting me with an awesome ministry where the man of God shared his testimony on God's crushing. Those were words I needed to hear during that time; knowing that if he went through it, I could too. That time of crushing was a divine connection to great men and women of God that poured into me through their ministry.

Another divine connection came in 2017 when I happened to come across Simply Agape Ministries on my

Facebook page. At the time I discovered it, I did not pay much attention to it, but God kept connecting my eyes and heart to look into this page. Eventually, I called their prayer line. I did this a few times sporadically, but every call was worth it as God used this line to help me through my crushing. Soon I became a faithful caller. God then directed me to enroll in a mentorship program headed by the founder and CEO of Simply Agape Ministries, Inc., Mother Andrea Carn. At the time that He told me to join the program, I didn't realize it but discovered that I was in a state of mild depression. I would just sleep, eat and be very moody. I could barely go to church. I would be up one day, and the next day I'm down. But thank God, for being God. He saw my state and my fight and connected me to a woman of God with an abundance of faith, a midwife, to help birth me out of my wilderness into my purpose towards my destiny. Through my mentorship with Mother, God showed me, by the unction of the Holy Ghost, everything in me that I did not realize was there. The first assignment she gave me was to journal daily. I recalled that during that first week of journaling, I was having a major pity party on paper. After reading my first week's journal entry, I said, "Suzette, if you call yourself a child of God and cannot trust God's word then you might as well throw in the towel." That Sunday I served the devil, my adversary, notice that "From this day forward you will not torment my mind. I am a child of God and I will stand on His word." That Monday morning while in prayer, God directed me to do forty days of fasting, prayer and consecration and to stay before Him. I was only to eat a light meal at 6 p.m. for those forty days. During this time, my faith began to increase by leaps and bounds. I started to learn who God was for myself and to build an authentic relationship with Him kicking religion out the door. It was through connecting with Mother Carn, who was inspired by God to be just what I needed in a mentor, and being on this forty days of fasting, prayer and consecration that I birthed this book, *Birthing Out Of My Wilderness*. I am forever grateful for the divine connection with Mother Carn, and the opportunity to write this 40-day devotional comprised of my daily journal entries and being inspired by God.

I pray this book will bless you and propel you into alignment with God to execute your purpose on Earth. We are all agents on a mission for God. He stated in Genesis 1:26-28, "Let us make man in our image, after our likeness: and let them have dominion over the fish of the sea, and over the fowl of the air, and over the cattle, and over all the earth, and over every creeping thing that creepeth upon the earth. So God created man in his *own* image, in the image of God created he him; male and female created he them. And God blessed them, and God said unto them, Be fruitful, and multiply, and replenish the earth, and subdue it: and have dominion over the fish of the sea, and over the fowl of the air, and over every living thing that moveth upon the earth." The Great Architect, God, has already mapped out the plan for our lives. Let's walk in the dominion, power and authority that He has given to us. He also said in Jeremiah

29:11 NIV, "For I know the plans I have for you, declares the Lord, plans to prosper you and not to harm you, plans to give you hope and a future." God has a great plan for each of our lives, and it is far beyond what we can imagine or dream. We can experience this life He has prepared by being in total alignment with Him.

INSTRUCTIONS

Before you start, inquire with our heavenly Father on the fast He desires for you. For this book to be beneficial to you, it is imperative that you include fasting, prayer and consecration each day. I have included a reflection page and a journal page after each day to document your thoughts. I encourage you to write down everything that the Lord speaks to you so that you can continue to meditate on it even after you have finished your 40-day fast. I also encourage you to enter this time with the Lord with an open heart and mind to be able to hear directly from Him and discover the wonderful plans He has for you. Allow our heavenly Father to renew your mind and realign the total you—spirit, soul and body—with Him

1

WHO AM I IN GOD?

I would ask myself this question from time to time, and I am sure you have done the same. What's my purpose on this Earth? Why did God give me life? After surrendering my all to God and desiring to build an authentic relationship with Him by putting away religious habits, (i.e., attending church religiously as a "routine," focusing on what I should NOT do instead of what I should do for God) I was able to answer that question. I am the apple of God's eye and He loves me unconditionally. He created me in His image and likeness, with a great plan to prosper me. He gave me dominion over all the earth, and He also said I should be fruitful and multiply, spiritually and naturally, to replenish the earth and that I should subdue it. God has given us the authority to do His work on Earth. We are considered "little gods" on Earth (see Psalm 8:5). God created each one of us unique, and we must take care of what He has entrusted to us, but our soulish desires separate us from His mission through us. We must look to God with an open heart, allowing Him to have total access, with no restraint, even when our natural eyes do not understand what's before us. God can do great things through us. That's who we are in God.

Suzette A. Fox

MEDITATE:

But he that is joined unto the Lord is one spirit.
1 Corinthians 6:17

I am complete in Him Who is the Head of all principality
and power. Colossians 2:10 (paraphrased)

But ye *are* a chosen generation, a royal priesthood, an holy
nation, a peculiar people; that ye should shew forth the
praises of him who hath called you out of darkness into his
marvellous light; which in time past *were* not a people, but
are now the people of God: which had not obtained mercy,
but now have obtained mercy. 1 Peter 2:9–10

It is of the LORD's mercies that we are not consumed,
because his compassions fail not. They are new every
morning: great is thy faithfulness. Lamentation 3:22-23

Faithful *is* he that calleth you, who also will do it.
1 Thessalonians 5:24

REFLECTION

Take some time to reflect on today's devotion.

Have you ever asked yourself, who you are in God and who God is in you?

_____

_____

_____

If yes, did today's devotion help you to answer your question?

_____

_____

_____

_____

_____

If no, did today's devotion confirm or enlighten your identity in God?

_____

_____

_____

_____

_____

Suzette A. Fox

NO ONE LEFT BEHIND

How can you guide someone to know their identity in God through today's devotion?

_____
_____
_____
_____
_____
_____
_____
_____
_____
_____
_____
_____
_____
_____
_____
_____
_____
_____
_____
_____
_____

Before I formed thee in the belly I knew thee; and before thou camest forth out of the womb I sanctified thee, *and* I ordained thee a prophet unto the nations.
Jeremiah 1:5

Suzette A. Fox

JOURNAL YOUR DAY

_____
_____
_____
_____
_____
_____
_____
_____
_____
_____
_____
_____
_____
_____
_____
_____
_____
_____
_____
_____
_____
_____
_____
_____
_____
_____
_____
_____
_____

Suzette A. Fox

_____

_____

_____

_____

_____

_____

_____

_____

_____

_____

_____

_____

_____

_____

_____

_____

_____

_____

_____

_____

_____

_____

_____

_____

_____

I am complete in Him Who is the Head of all principality and power.
Colossians 2:10 (paraphrased)

2

HE'S A GOOD FATHER

How do we know that God is a good father? Because He first loved us with no condition, no condemnation, or no self-motive. He loved us even when we did not love ourselves. We may say we always loved ourselves, but I beg the differ. When we were living in sin, the devil made us think we were living life, but he was sabotaging our real lives in so many ways by allowing destruction to dilute our minds. He wanted us to think that destroying our lives was the plan God had for us. But God robed himself in flesh and sacrificed Himself as a Lamb on the cross through Jesus Christ to redeem us from our sin. He did this to set the captive free from bondage and to give us a new life. In the Old Testament they sacrificed the lamb for the atonement of their sins, but in the New Testament it was His son, Jesus, who was robed in flesh and walked among men and they knew him not. However, today God has called us to be born again of the water and of the Holy Spirit to enter into the Kingdom of God which is only the first step. God desires to take care of us wholeheartedly with all the promises He has for us. In order for Him to do so, we have to surrender our all to Him, in faith, and trust Him with the life He has given us. God has so much for us, but we will never know until we trust Him.

Suzette A. Fox

MEDITATE:

Behold, what manner of love the Father hath bestowed upon us, that we should be called the sons of God: therefore the world knoweth us not, because it knew him not. 1John 3:1

But now, O Lord, thou _art_ our father; we _are_ the clay, and thou our potter; and we all _are_ the work of thy hand. Isaiah 64:8

That thine alms may be in secret: and thy Father which seeth in secret himself shall reward thee openly. Matthew 6:4

Have not I commanded thee? Be strong and of a good courage; be not afraid, neither be thou dismayed: for the LORD thy God is with thee whithersoever thou goest. Joshua 1:9

Like as a father pitieth his children, so the LORD pitieth them that fear him. Psalm 103:13

REFLECTION

Take some time to reflect on today's devotion.

Did today's devotion clarify whom the Father, God, is too you?

_____

_____

If yes, what *were* the areas in your life you had doubts about His ability to be your Father?

_____

_____

_____

_____

_____

If no, what *are* the areas in your life you have doubts of His ability to be your father?

_____

_____

_____

_____

_____

_____

Suzette A. Fox

If you responded no, find a sentence or scripture in the devotion to add to your daily prayer. As you pray, believe with your heart that it is so.

NO ONE LEFT BEHIND

Now that you have prayed and are trusting in God's word that He is a good Father; how can you guide someone to know that God loves them and desires to father them?

_____

_____

_____

_____

_____

_____

_____

_____

_____

_____

_____

_____

_____

_____

_____

But now, O Lord, thou *art* our father; we *are* the clay, and thou our potter; and we all *are* the work of thy hand.
Isaiah 64:8

JOURNAL YOUR DAY

_____
_____
_____
_____
_____
_____
_____
_____
_____
_____
_____
_____
_____
_____
_____
_____
_____
_____
_____
_____
_____
_____
_____

Suzette A. Fox

_____

_____

_____

_____

_____

_____

_____

_____

_____

_____

_____

_____

_____

_____

_____

_____

_____

_____

_____

_____

_____

_____

_____

Like as a father pitieth *his* children, *so* the Lord pitieth them that fear him.

Psalm 103:13

12

3

GOD, OUR PROVIDER

God is our Jehovah Jireh. He is always ready to provide for us. Not trusting God will always separate us from all of His provision. Abraham trusted that God would send him a ram when God directed him to take his son whom he loved dearly, Isaac, to Mount Moriah for a sacrifice. Moses and Aaron trusted that God would lead and direct them when they had to face Pharaoh with God's messages to let His people go. They also had to trust that He would provide for them as they journeyed through the wilderness to the Promised Land. I had to come to a place of trusting God and knowing that He would provide all of my needs. When I did not have the money to pay my mortgage, I wanted to sell my house, but God said, "Wait." When God directed me to leave Amazon and drive for Uber, my car was at the mechanics more than it was on the road, but God made sure that all my bills were paid. I didn't experience any insufficiency in my bank account. When He directed me to work only five hours a day and spend the rest of my time with Him, He gave me the grace to do so. He kept his hand on all my possession and gave my children and I an abundance of favor. God will provide for us only if we walk in His will. Our blessings are merely a by-product of our obedience to Him. Would you trust Him to provide for you?

Suzette A. Fox

MEDITATE:

He raiseth up the poor out of the dust, *and* lifteth up the beggar from the dunghill, to set *them* among princes, and to make them inherit the throne of glory: for the pillars of the earth *are* the Lord's, and he hath set the world upon them. 1 Samuel 2:8

Both riches and honour *come* of thee, and thou reignest over all; and in thine hand *is* power and might; and in thine hand *it is* to make great, and to give strength unto all. 1 Chronicles 29:12

But my God shall supply all your need according to his riches in glory by Christ Jesus. Philippians 4:19

And Abraham said, My son, God will provide himself a lamb for a burnt offering: so they went both of them together. Genesis 22:7

REFLECTION

Take some time to reflect on today's devotion.

What are your thoughts on today's devotion of trusting God to provide for you?

_____

_____

_____

_____

Were there any doubts prior to now of God being your provider?

_____

_____

_____

_____

If yes, what do you believe caused those doubts, and how can you correct them?

_____

_____

_____

_____

If no, what were your strategies to strengthen that area in your spiritual walk?

_____

_____

_____

_____

_____

_____

No one left behind

How can you guide or teach someone that God's desire is to be their provider?

_____

_____

_____

_____

_____

_____

_____

_____

_____

_____

_____

_____

_____

_____

_____

_____

_____

For thou, Lord, wilt bless the righteous; with favour wilt thou compass him as *with* a shield. Psalm 5:12

JOURNAL YOUR DAY

_____
_____
_____
_____
_____
_____
_____
_____
_____
_____
_____
_____
_____
_____
_____
_____
_____
_____
_____
_____
_____
_____
_____
_____
_____
_____
_____
_____

Suzette A. Fox

_____
_____
_____
_____
_____
_____
_____
_____
_____
_____
_____
_____
_____
_____
_____
_____
_____
_____
_____
_____
_____
_____
_____
_____
_____

But my God shall supply all your need according to his riches in glory by Christ Jesus.
Philippians 4:19

4

GOD IS SPEAKING
ARE WE LISTENING?

God is always speaking, but because of our busy lives, we can often miss what He's saying. God desires to communicate with us at all times. His communication consists of giving us direction, protection, His love, and showing us things within us that are not pleasing to Him. He is always trying to get His very best to us and to do that He'll speak to us through wise counsel, our circumstances or through His peace. Colossians 3:15 says, "And let the peace of God rule in your hearts, to the which also ye are called in one body; and be ye thankful." God can speak to us through many ways including dreams, vision, and prophecy (Acts 2:17), our thoughts (Matthew 1:19–21), natural manifestations (John 12:27–30), and supernatural manifestations (Exodus 3:1–4). He primarily speaks to us through the Bible or His word (Hebrew 4:12), but He can also speak to us through a whisper (1 Kings 19:12). We must start our day with God so that we can hear from Him throughout the day. We are always on an assignment for God, but if we are not focused like an eagle, we can miss many of the opportunities He assigns to us to pray for His people, speak a word into someone's life, assist someone in need, or even fulfill our long-term assignment through Him.

Suzette A. Fox

MEDITATE:

And there came a voice from heaven, *saying*, Thou art my beloved Son, in whom I am well pleased. Mark 1:11

But the voice answered me again from heaven, What God hath cleansed, *that* call not thou common. Acts 11:9

Out of heaven he made thee to hear his voice, that he might instruct thee: and upon earth he shewed thee his great fire; and thou hearest his words out of the midst of the fire. Deuteronomy 4:36

But he said, Yea rather, blessed are they that hear the word of God, and keep it. Luke 11:28

So then faith *cometh* by hearing, and hearing by the word of God. Romans 10:17

REFLECTION

Take some time to reflect on today's devotion.

Did today's devotion bring any awareness of the importance of listening to God's direction?

_____

_____

_____

_____

_____

If yes, is there any assignment God has given you, but you are still in doubt?

_____

_____

_____

_____

Assignment: List your assignments, go to our Father in prayer and ask for faith, guidance, divine connections, power and authority to overcome all negative responses. Stay before the Father until you are strengthened in this area.

If no, list why you feel that it's not important to listen to God's direction.

_____

_____

_____

Suzette A. Fox

_____

_____

_____

_____

_____

_____

Assignment: Pray daily that Holy Spirit will open up your understanding on the importance of listening and obeying His directions.

NO ONE LEFT BEHIND

Now that you have a better understanding and are confident in listening and obeying God's direction, how can you guide and teach someone else?

_____

_____

_____

_____

_____

_____

_____

_____

_____

My sheep hear my voice, and I know them, and they follow me.
John 10:27

JOURNAL YOUR DAY

_____
_____
_____
_____
_____
_____
_____
_____
_____
_____
_____
_____
_____
_____
_____
_____
_____
_____
_____
_____
_____
_____
_____
_____
_____
_____
_____
_____

Suzette A. Fox

_____

_____

_____

_____

_____

_____

_____

_____

_____

_____

_____

_____

_____

_____

_____

_____

_____

_____

_____

_____

_____

_____

_____

_____

_____

Then shall ye call upon me, and ye shall go and pray unto me, and I will hearken unto you. Jeremiah 29:12

5

HIS UNCONDITIONAL LOVE

"For God so loved the world, that he gave his only begotten Son, that whosoever believeth in him should not perish, but have everlasting life" (John 3:16). God's love is unconditional. Even with our sinful nature, He loves us but He hates sin which separates us from Him. God loves us so much that He gave us a free will (soul) so that we could choose for ourselves who would we love. Some have chosen to love themselves, the world, material things or to love God just to receive His blessing, while others have chosen to love God unconditionally. The love of God is very pure and rich, and although some choose not to love Him, He still desires to love them in spite of their choice. No one else could have made the sacrifice that was required, but He did by being robed in flesh and walking among men. God came Himself in the person of Jesus Christ to fulfill what no one else could. The Bible says that "without controversy great is the mystery of godliness: God was manifested in the flesh, justified in the Spirit, seen of angels, preached unto the Gentiles, believed on in the world, received up into glory" (1 Timothy 3:16). And even when they rejected Him, He did not allow their action to dictate His action or keep Him from going on the cross for our sins. The Bible tells us that "He was in the world, and the world was made by him, and the world knew him not" (John 1:10). God has left these

Suzette A. Fox

examples for us to love unconditionally, even when we are rejected by others or treated unfairly. We have to allow His light to shine through us as He did when He walked among men.

MEDITATE:

Greater love hath no man than this, that a man lay down his life for his friends. John 15:13

But God commendeth his love toward us, in that, while we were yet sinners, Christ died for us. Romans 5:8

But thou, O Lord, *art* a God full of compassion, and gracious, long suffering, and plenteous in mercy and truth. Psalm 86:15

Cause me to hear thy lovingkindness in the morning; for in thee do I trust: cause me to know the way wherein I should walk; for I lift up my soul unto thee. Psalm 143:8

26

Suzette A. Fox

REFLECTION

Take some time to reflect on today's devotion.

Throughout your day, were you able to embrace God's unconditional love?

_____

_____

_____

If yes, what were those areas, and how were you able to embrace His unconditional love?

_____

_____

_____

_____

_____

_____

_____

_____

_____

_____

If no, what prevented you from embracing and understanding His unconditional love and what method can you use to change your mindset?

_____

_____

_____

_____

_____

_____

_____

No One Left Behind

Now that you have a better understanding of God's unconditional love, how can you exercise this love toward others and also teach them in doing so?

_____

_____

_____

_____

_____

_____

_____

_____

_____

_____

_____

_____

But I say unto you which hear, Love your enemies, do good to them which hate you.
Luke 6:27

JOURNAL YOUR DAY

_____
_____
_____
_____
_____
_____
_____
_____
_____
_____
_____
_____
_____
_____
_____
_____
_____
_____
_____
_____
_____
_____
_____
_____
_____
_____
_____

Suzette A. Fox

_____

_____

_____

_____

_____

_____

_____

_____

_____

_____

_____

_____

_____

_____

_____

_____

_____

_____

_____

_____

_____

_____

The Lord hath appeared of old unto me, *saying*, Yea, I have loved thee with an
everlasting love: therefore with lovingkindness have I drawn thee.
Jeremiah 31:3

6

FORGIVENESS

"Bear with each other and forgive one another if any of you has a grievance against someone. Forgive as the Lord forgave you" (Colossians 3:13 NIV).

Unforgiveness, metaphorically, is a cancer cell that can cause tumors to manifest in your mind, body and soul. When you forgive, you are setting yourself free from being a slave to your perpetrator in your mind. Holding on to something that someone has done to you can cause you to be stuck in the era of where the initial incident occurred while they go on with their life. Holding unforgiveness is not beneficial to you or your health. It causes sickness to the heart, which is the central organ of our body, which in turn may cause other areas of our bodies to be affected. Forgiveness is a choice. Before I learned how to draw near to God, I did not know how to forgive and would hold a grudge for years. As I drew closer to Him, God's love eradicated these "cancer cells" of unforgiveness out of my heart, and His love made me whole again. I stayed before God day and night, crying out to Him to consume all unforgiveness from my heart as I called out the names of those I needed to forgive. God once gave me a dream of a couple from my church showing me how He had blessed them. I asked the couple why they were so happy, and they replied, "God just blessed us with a five-bedroom house!" I then heard the Lord say to me in the dream "I desire to do the same, if only you forgive." Unforgiveness separates us from God like any other sin. It also affects our intimacy with Him. In that dream, God also said to me, "Forgiveness is a choice," which was the solution to the problem. I then positioned my mind and heart to let go of any unforgiveness and set the person(s) free from my mind and heart. The method to forgive is to love the offender with the love of God.

MEDITATE:

And be ye kind one to another, tenderhearted, forgiving one another, even as God for Christ's sake hath forgiven you. Ephesians 4:32

For if ye forgive men their trespasses, your heavenly Father will also forgive you: But if ye forgive not men their trespasses, neither will your father forgive your trespasses. Matthew 6:14–15

Forbearing one another, and forgiving one another, if any man have a quarrel against any: even as Christ forgave you, so also do ye. Colossians 3:13

Judge not, and ye shall not be judged: condemn not, and ye shall not be condemned: forgive, and ye shall be forgiven. Luke 6:37

REFLECTION

Take some time to reflect on today's devotion.

As you reflect on your day and life, is there anyone you need to forgive? Please take this time to be very honest with yourself and search your heart with prayer.

_____

_____

List the names of those you need to forgive and the nature of the offense.

_____

_____

_____

_____

_____

_____

_____

Assignment: In your daily prayer take these names and the offense to the Father. Expose your heart to Him. There is no need to hold back because He already knows your heart and desires to free you from this stronghold. Do not cease from this prayer until you know in your heart you have released all offenders to God and freed yourself. Be sure to pray for them in love and also ask the Father to forgive you of any offense toward them.

Suzette A. Fox

Now let's test your spirit.

Take your mind back to the offense. How do you feel? Is there, anger, hurt, or hateful thoughts? If yes, continue to stay before the Father until you know that when you see or hear about the offender, you can embrace them with love— God's unconditional love. NOW YOU HAVE WON THE BATTLE!

NO ONE LEFT BEHIND

Now that you have conquered unforgiveness, how can you teach someone else what you have learned about forgiving others with the love of God?

_____

_____

_____

_____

_____

_____

_____

_____

_____

_____

_____

_____

For if ye forgive men their trespasses, your heavenly Father will also forgive you.
Matthew 6:14

JOURNAL YOUR DAY

Suzette A. Fox

_____
_____
_____
_____
_____
_____
_____
_____
_____
_____
_____
_____
_____
_____
_____
_____
_____
_____
_____
_____
_____
_____
_____
_____

But if ye forgive not men their trespasses, neither will your Father forgive your
trespasses. Matthew 6:15

7

SOUL TIES

A person's soul can be described as someone's moral emotions or sense of identity. A soul tie occurs when two individual's souls are tied together in a relationship in the spirit realm. A godly soul tie is established only through divine encounters set up by God and include friendships, business relationships or marriage. Ephesians 5:31 states, "For this cause shall a man leave his father and mother, and shall be joined unto his wife, and they two shall be one flesh." An ungodly soul tie is often established through fornication, adultery or any unhealthy sinful relationship or desire. When someone is involved in sexual relations without marriage, or a person begins to idolize someone they have connected to in a close business or friendship, a soul ties can be formed. From this we can see that some soul ties are good, and some are not. It all depends on how the relationship was formed and the motive of the individuals in the relationship. Let's take a look at Jonathan and David's relationship in 1 Samuel 18:1. "And it came to pass, when he had made an end of speaking unto Saul, that the soul of Jonathan was knit with the soul of David, and Jonathan loved him as his own soul." Their relationship is an example of one that God brought together divinely, and as a result, they had a soul tie orchestrated by God. If you find yourself in relationships that God did not ordain, you need to seek

His help in breaking any soul ties that you may have formed knowingly or unknowingly. To break ungodly soul ties, start by repenting to God. You may also need to return all gifts and possessions that you have received or anything symbolic of your relationship because those can keep you connected to the person. Renounce- any commitments or non-marital vows you may have made with the person. It is important to speak words of life over your relationships and discontinue using phrases such as, "I can't live without them," or "I'll love this person forever." Change your thoughts regarding that person but don't hold any unforgiveness. Break the soul tie in the name of Jesus and forgive the person and yourself with the love of God. Seek God for the relationships that He has planned for you.

Suzette A. Fox

MEDITATE:

Be ye not unequally yoked together with unbelievers: for what fellowship hath righteousness with unrighteousness? and what communion hath light with darkness?
2 Corinthians 6:14

Flee fornication. Every sin that a man doeth is without the body; but he that committeth fornication sinneth against his own body. 1 Corinthians 6:18

And the very God of peace sanctify you wholly; and I pray God your whole spirit and soul and body be preserved blameless unto the coming of our Lord Jesus Christ.
1 Thessalonians 5:23

REFLECTION

Take some time to reflect on today's devotion.

As you reflect, are there any ungodly soul ties that need to be broken?

_____

_____

_____

_____

List the names of the people you may have an ungodly soul tie with and take it to the Father in prayer, believing that God can and will release you from every soul tie.

_____

_____

_____

_____

_____

_____

_____

_____

Note: Do not cease from praying until you know that it is broken.

Now that every soul tie is broken, walk in God's love and allow Him to divinely connect you with whom He desires.

Suzette A. Fox

No one left behind

Now that you have allowed God to break those ungodly soul ties, use your testimony to help someone else.

_____

_____

_____

_____

_____

_____

_____

_____

_____

_____

_____

_____

_____

_____

_____

_____

_____

_____

_____

_____

_____

_____

Be ye not unequally yoked together with unbelievers: for what fellowship hath righteousness with unrighteousness? and what communion hath light with darkness?   2 Corinthians 6:14

JOURNAL YOUR DAY

Suzette A. Fox

_____
_____
_____
_____
_____
_____
_____
_____
_____
_____
_____
_____
_____
_____
_____
_____
_____
_____
_____
_____
_____
_____
_____
_____
_____

And the very God of peace sanctify you wholly; and I pray God your whole spirit and
soul and body be preserved blameless unto the coming of our Lord Jesus Christ.
1 Thessalonians 5:23

8

GOSSIP

To gossip is to engage in casual or constrained conversation or repeat reports about other people that you have heard. God is never pleased when we gossip and tear down our brothers and sisters especially when we should be building each other up. Gossip will cause you to have impaired judgement, anger, hatred, disappointment and bring discord amongst brethren. God is not a proponent of this activity going on in the church and speaks of it in the Bible, "A perverse person stirs up conflict, and a gossip separates close friends" (Proverbs 16:28 NIV). I once enjoyed sitting in the company of gossipers which is just as bad as being the one who starts the gossip. The word of God said, "Let no unwholesome word proceed from your mouth, but only such a word as is good for edification according to the need of the moment, so that it will give grace to those who hear" (Ephesians 4:29). Unfortunately, some within the Body of Christ believe it's ok, but it's not. We have to sanctify ourselves from the things of this world and allow God to create in us a clean heart and renew a right spirit within us. (Psalm 51:10) When we allow His word to transform us by the renewing of our mind, gossip has got go.

MEDITATE:

A froward man soweth strife: and a whisperer separateth chief friends. Proverbs 16:28

Thou shalt not raise a false report: put not thine hand with the wicked to be an unrighteous witness. Exodus 23:1

If any man among you seem to be religious, and bridleth not his tongue, but deceiveth his own heart, this man's religion is vain. James 1:26

Thou shalt not bear false witness against thy neighbour. Exodus 20:16

Suzette A. Fox

REFLECTION

Take some time to reflect on today's devotion.

As you reflect over your day, were you entangled in any gossip?

_____

_____

_____

_____

If yes, how would you refrain from any type of gossip, now that we know it's displeasing to God?

_____

_____

_____

_____

_____

_____

_____

If no, what's your strategy to continue to refrain from gossip?

_____

_____

_____

_____

Suzette A. Fox

_____

_____

_____

_____

NO ONE LEFT BEHIND

What can you do to teach others the importance of refraining from gossip?

_____

_____

_____

_____

_____

_____

_____

_____

_____

_____

_____

_____

_____

_____

_____

A talebearer revealeth secrets: but he that is of a faithful spirit concealeth the matter.   Proverbs 11:13

JOURNAL YOUR DAY

Suzette A. Fox

_____

_____

_____

_____

_____

_____

_____

_____

_____

_____

_____

_____

_____

_____

_____

_____

_____

_____

_____

_____

_____

_____

_____

_____

Thou shalt not raise a false report: put not thine hand with the wicked to be an unrighteous witness.   Exodus 23:1

9

THE TONGUE

"Death and life *are* in the power of the tongue: and they that love it shall eat the fruit thereof" (Proverbs 18:21). The Bible speaks of the importance of watching what comes out of our mouths, but it also speaks on guarding our hearts because what we speak, comes from our hearts. When our heart is pure, our speech will be pure. Proverbs 4:23 says, that we must, "keep [our] heart with all diligence; for out of it *are* the issues of life." Jesus said it well in Matthew 12:34, "O generation of vipers, how can ye, being evil, speak good things? for out of the abundance of the heart the mouth speaketh." Solomon also had a few words to say about this matter in Proverbs 16:23, "The heart of the wise teacheth his mouth, and addeth learning to his lips." It's imperative to pray always and allow God to search our hearts. There may be things hidden that we didn't realize were in our hearts like unforgiveness, anger, hatred, impatience, backbiting, idolatry, pride, tale-bearing, and gossip. God desires to consume everything in us that is ungodly or carnal by fire and wash our hearts with His word. Psalm 51:10 says, "Create in [us] a clean heart, O God; and renew a right spirit within [us]." I recalled one time during a particularly trying time where I would fight with my tongue. But God arrested me with Psalm 39:1, "I will take heed to my ways, that I sin not with my tongue: I will keep my mouth with a bridle, while the wicked is before me." In other words, God was letting me know to zip my mouth, bridle my tongue and He will fight my battles.

MEDITATE:

For he that will love life, and see good days, let him refrain his tongue from evil, and his lips that they speak no guile.
1 Peter 3:10

Let your speech *be* always with grace, seasoned with salt, that ye may know how ye ought to answer every man.
Colossians 4:6

Let no corrupt communication proceed out of your mouth, but that which is good to the use of edifying, that it may minister grace unto the hearers.
Ephesians 4:29

REFLECTION

Take some time to reflect on today's devotion.

What are your thoughts on today's devotion?

_____

_____

_____

_____

_____

Were you tested with your tongue today?

_____

_____

_____

_____

If yes, were you able to refrain from using your tongue as a weapon, and did you correct your action with God and the person?

_____

_____

_____

_____

_____

_____

_____

If you continue to struggle in this area, be sure to never cease from praying to our Father to give you the strength, wisdom and understanding and most importantly to stand on His word. He will fight your battle.

NO ONE LEFT BEHIND

Now that you have conquered bridling your tongue and pleasing God, how can you teach someone else to do the same?

_____

_____

_____

_____

_____

_____

_____

_____

_____

_____

_____

_____

_____

_____

_____

_____

Whoso keepeth his mouth and his tongue, keepeth his soul from troubles.
Proverbs 21:23

JOURNAL YOUR DAY

Suzette A. Fox

_____
_____
_____
_____
_____
_____
_____
_____
_____
_____
_____
_____
_____
_____
_____
_____
_____
_____
_____
_____
_____
_____
_____
_____
_____

For he that will love life, and see good days, let him refrain his tongue from evil, and
his lips that they speak no guile.
1 Peter 3:10

10

HUMILITY

Humility is defined as lowliness, meekness, modesty, or being down to earth. Pride, on the other hand, is associated with showy, overly-impressive, disdainful behavior. When we approach God, we have to understand that we can't come before Him with pride. God will not accept our worship nor our praise if we bring pride in His presence. Pride comes in many forms and when our desire is for God to reshape us into His image and likeness, it can't be with a "look at me," or "all eyes on me" approach. It's imperative to approach God with a humble heart, a heart of flesh desiring to be broken to meekness and lowliness. He will take away a stony heart (Ezekiel 36:26) and replace it with a heart that is desiring to express the fruit of the spirit. Galatians 5:22–23 says, "But the fruit of the Spirit is love, joy, peace, longsuffering, gentleness, goodness, faith, Meekness, temperance: against such there is no law." Humility allows God to have His liberty with us, and He will show us what's hidden in our heart, and how He views us in His eyes, with no condemnation. Humility will always bring us to a place of repentance, a place of "a broken spirit: a broken and a contrite heart" (Psalm 51:17). Humility also brings us into an intimate place with God.

Suzette A. Fox

MEDITATE:

With all lowliness and meekness, with longsuffering, forbearing one another in love. Ephesians 4:2

Let nothing be done through strife or vainglory; but in lowliness of mind let each esteem other better than themselves. Philippians 2:3

Be of the same mind one toward another. Mind not high things, but condescend to men of low estate. Be not wise in your own conceits. Romans 12:16

Humble yourselves in the sight of the Lord, and he shall lift you up. James 4:10

REFLECTION

Take some time to reflect on today's devotion.

Reflect on your thoughts regarding what humility means to you.

_____

_____

_____

_____

_____

_____

As you search your heart, do you believe you have a humble spirit according to the word of God?

_____

_____

_____

_____

_____

_____

_____

_____

_____

_____

_____

_____

If your heart is humble, I encourage you to continue to allow God to keep your spirit humble.

If it's not, seek our Father for His guidance in uprooting any spirit of pride. Allow the word of God to teach you how to be of a humble spirit.

NO ONE LEFT BEHIND

Now that you have conquered pride and are preserving a humble spirit, how can you teach someone else the importance of humility?

_____

_____

_____

_____

_____

_____

_____

_____

_____

_____

_____

_____

When pride cometh, then cometh shame: but with the lowly *is* wisdom.
Proverbs 11:2

JOURNAL YOUR DAY

Suzette A. Fox

_____
_____
_____
_____
_____
_____
_____
_____
_____
_____
_____
_____
_____
_____
_____
_____
_____
_____
_____
_____
_____
_____
_____
_____
_____

With all lowliness and meekness, with longsuffering, forbearing one another in love.   Ephesians 4:2

11

FEAR NOT

Fear and doubt are delusional giants that stifle the forward progress of anyone but in particular in the children of God. Fear and doubt attack the heart and mind of believers to try to stop them from becoming bold because the great accuser, the devil, knows what will happen. He will no longer have any control over us to prevent us from executing God's plan. Once we rise in boldness, the enemy can no longer control us with the delusion that we can't accomplish something big for God. In every assignment that God gives us, it's imperative that we put all of our trust in Him knowing that it is not us doing the work, but God working through us. We make ourselves available for His use as earthen vessels. Fear can be conquered through worship and brings us to an intimate place with God. To worship God freely and fearlessly, we have to know who we are in Him and who He is in us. If we don't, fear can tend to reside within us. When there is fear in your heart, it can open the door to a religious spirit where you think that God has a lot of "do not do's" that you have to live your life by. However, He is a God that is interested in us "doing," meaning that when you read His Word are we going to "do" what His word says. When we do what His word says to do, it brings us to a place of intimacy. His word says, "For God hath not given us the spirit of fear: but of power, and of love, and of a sound

64

Suzette A. Fox

mind" (2 Timothy 1:7). But how can we conquer fear and doubt that may be hiding in our hearts? Prayer and fasting are at the top of the list. However, we can also conquer this delusional giant by doing the opposite of what our minds may be telling us to do and stepping out in faith and do what God says. That was my strategy to conquer fear. Now I can walk in power and authority with a sound mind and with love to execute His plan.

MEDITATE:

The Lord *is* my light and my salvation; whom shall I fear? the Lord *is* the strength of my life; of whom shall I be afraid? Psalm 27:1

Fear thou not; for I *am* with thee: be not dismayed; for I *am* thy God: I will strengthen thee; yea, I will help thee; yea, I will uphold thee with the right hand of my righteousness. Isaiah 41:10

REFLECTION

Take some time to reflect on today's devotion.

What are your thoughts on fear?

_____

_____

_____

_____

What are you fearful of?

_____

_____

_____

_____

Note: Take those things that you are fearful of to our Father in prayer and do not cease from praying until you build your strength, by faith, to face those fears.

As you reflect on today's devotion, do you have the confidence to stand on God's word to conquer the spirit of fear?

_____

_____

_____

_____

_____

_____

If no, I encourage you to stay before our Father in prayer to build your faith in Him to kill the spirit of fear.

If yes, I celebrate with you as you stand bold in faith to execute all that God has assigned you to do.

NO ONE LEFT BEHIND

Now that you have conquered the spirit of fear and are walking in your assignments, how can you teach and help someone else do the same?

_____

_____

_____

_____

_____

_____

_____

_____

_____

_____

_____

_____

_____

_____

In the multitude of my thoughts within me thy comforts delight my soul.
Psalm 94:19

Suzette A. Fox

JOURNAL YOUR DAY

_____
_____
_____
_____
_____
_____
_____
_____
_____
_____
_____
_____
_____
_____
_____
_____
_____
_____
_____
_____
_____
_____
_____
_____
_____

Suzette A. Fox

_____
_____
_____
_____
_____
_____
_____
_____
_____
_____
_____
_____
_____
_____
_____
_____
_____
_____
_____
_____
_____
_____
_____
_____

Peace I leave with you, my peace I give unto you: not as the world giveth, give I
unto you. Let not your heart be troubled, neither let it be afraid.
John 14:27

12

FEARLESS

Now that we have conquered the spirit of fear, it's now time to be FEARLESS and walk in the power and authority that God has given to us. God stated in Genesis 1:26, "And let them have dominion over the fish of the sea and over the fowl of the air, and over the cattle, and over all the earth, and over every creeping thing that creepeth upon the earth." Dominion pertains to having control, power, authority, giving a command or having superiority over all things. When God sends us on a mission, there is no need to allow fear, that delusional giant, to cripple us because He said He has given us dominion. Exercise His word by speaking life into your lives and the lives of others. God posed an interesting question to Ezekiel in Ezekiel 37:3, and in turn, Ezekiel answered Him, "Son of man, can these bones live? And I answered, O Lord God, thou knowest." Ezekiel was being fearless and walking in his power and authority, knowing God's word to be true. God then said to Ezekiel in Ezekiel 37:4, "Prophesy upon these bones, and say unto them, O ye dry bones, hear the word of the Lord. Thus saith the Lord God unto these bones; Behold, I will cause breath to enter into you, and he shall live." Ezekiel was once again fearless, he did not speak to those bones in his emotions, but he spoke what the Spirit of the Lord said with all power and authority. He did not look at what was before him, he looked

70

at the word of God and then stood on the word of God. We are fearless when we allow God and His word to work through us with all power and authority.

MEDITATE:

Though an host should encamp against me, my heart shall not fear: though war should rise against me, in this *will* I be confident. Psalm 27:3

Thou shalt not be afraid for the terror by night; *nor* for the arrow *that* flieth by day. Psalm 91:5

The Lord *is* on my side; I will not fear: what can man do unto me? Psalm 118:6

REFLECTION

Take some time to reflect on today's devotion.

What are your thoughts on the power and authority given to you?

_____

_____

Do you believe you can now walk in that power and authority?

_____

_____

_____

If yes, how would you challenge yourself in keeping your momentum?

_____

_____

_____

If no, what are your thoughts as to how you can build yourself up to increase your momentum?

_____

_____

_____

I encourage you to continue meditating on the scriptures given and also search for other related scriptures. Take those scriptures in prayer and allow the word to permeate into your heart, believing God's word in its entirety and then see God transform you by the renewing of your mind to walk FEARLESS.

No One Left Behind

Now that you are walking in the power and authority that is given to you, how can you teach someone else to do the same?

_____

_____

_____

_____

_____

_____

_____

_____

_____

_____

_____

_____

_____

Being confident of this very thing, that he which hath begun a good work in you will perform *it* until the day of Jesus Christ.
Philippians 1:6

JOURNAL YOUR DAY

Suzette A. Fox

_____
_____
_____
_____
_____
_____
_____
_____
_____
_____
_____
_____
_____
_____
_____
_____
_____
_____
_____
_____
_____
_____
_____

Take therefore no thought for the morrow: for the morrow shall take thought for
the things of itself. Sufficient unto the day *is* the evil thereof.
Matthew 6:34

13

FAITH AS A MUSTARD SEED

I was taught that faith is knowing who God is. How can we know who God is? Through His word. The word of God declares, "In the beginning was the Word, and the Word was with God, and the Word was God" (John 1:1). God created the world and man by faith. He spoke the word, and it happened. And because of this example, we can follow his boldness and speak the word, regardless of what we see with our natural eyes. God designed us to be like Him, and there is only one way to get results the same way He does. Speak the word only. One word from the Lord can change your life, as stated in Ezekiel 37:4-5, "Again he said unto me, Prophesy upon these bones, and say unto them, O ye dry bones, hear the word of the Lord. Thus saith the Lord God unto these bones; Behold, I will cause breath to enter into you, and ye shall live." Ezekiel did not look at these bones through his natural eyes but through his spiritual eyes to trust what God was saying. He was metaphorically speaking of the people of Israel, who turned their hearts away from God and once they did, their spirit man was dead to God. What's dead in your life that you're looking at only through your natural lenses? God is saying to you today, "Look through your spiritual lenses" and speak His word with boldness from your heart, that your situation will live according to the will of God. Are you praying for a rebellious child? I decree they shall live again. Are your finances at a substantial low? I speak life to your circumstances and that you are rising out of poverty and you and your household shall never suffer lack again as a child of God. Is there sickness in your body? I command every sickness to leave your body, and by His stripes, you are healed. I speak an abundance of hope and joy in your life. God's word will give us the strength to stand as a strong soldier in the army of the Lord to do His will. I speak the spirit of faith upon your life and that you shall never doubt the word of God again! You shall live and not die. Trust God and never give up!

Suzette A. Fox

MEDITATE:

If any of you lack wisdom, let him ask of God, that giveth to all *men* liberally, and upbraideth not; and it shall be given him. But let him ask in faith, nothing wavering. For he that wavereth is like a wave of the sea driven with the wind and tossed.   James 1:5-6

But the scripture hath concluded all under sin, that the promise by faith of Jesus Christ might be given to them that believe. But before faith came, we were kept under the law, shut up unto the faith which should afterwards be revealed. Wherefore the law was our schoolmaster to bring us unto Christ, that we might be justified by faith. But after that faith is come, we are no longer under a schoolmaster.
Galatians 3: 22-25

I am crucified with Christ: nevertheless I live; yet not I, but Christ liveth in me: and the life which I now live in the flesh I live by the faith of the Son of God, who loved me, and gave himself for me. I do not frustrate the grace of God: for if righteousness come by the law, then Christ is dead in vain.
Galatians 2:20-21

REFLECTION

Take some time to reflect on today's devotion.

What are your thoughts on faith as a mustard seed?

_____

_____

_____

_____

_____

_____

_____

What areas of your faith life are stronger than others?

_____

_____

_____

_____

_____

_____

How can you have a balance in your faith, where you trust God no matter the circumstance?

_____

_____

_____

Suzette A. Fox

_____

_____

_____

_____

Step by step, view life through the lens of God's word. Trust in His word and do not lean to your own understanding.

NO ONE LEFT BEHIND
How can you teach someone else what it means to walk by faith?

_____

_____

_____

_____

_____

_____

_____

_____

_____

_____

_____

_____

Trust in the Lord with all thine heart; and lean not unto thine own understanding. In all thy ways acknowledge him, and he shall direct thy paths.

Proverbs 3:5-6

JOURNAL YOUR DAY

Suzette A. Fox

_____

_____

_____

_____

_____

_____

_____

_____

_____

_____

_____

_____

_____

_____

_____

_____

_____

_____

_____

_____

_____

_____

_____

But as many as received him, to them gave he power to become the sons of God,
even to them that believe on his name.
John 1:12

14

WAR OVER YOUR PROPHECY

The enemy shows up in a believer's life to steal, kill and destroy. It's imperative, as Christians, that we war over our prophecy or our promise from God. As stated in Daniel 10:13, "But the prince of the kingdom of Persia withstood me one and twenty days: but, lo, Michael, one of the chief princes, came to help me; and I remained there with the kings of Persia." Daniel had a vision and a prophecy from God that after he prayed over Jerusalem's transgression, they would have peace. The angel of the Lord came to console Daniel after hearing his prayer, pleading for the lives of the people. Daniel had fasted for twenty-one days and the angel, Gabriel, heard his cry while he was on his way to Daniel with a message. During the twenty-one days, Gabriel had been held up in the second heaven by the prince of the kingdom of Persia, but Daniel kept his heart pure before God with persistence in prayer and consecration. Gabriel was not able to fight the forces of darkness alone, so he had to sanction the warring angel, Michael, to push back the evil forces to give Gabriel clearance to get to Daniel with the message. What this story tells us is that whatever vision or prophecy God has given you, never give up on it although it may take a while to manifest. Be sensitive just as Daniel was and stay in a position of alertness to fast, pray or consecrate yourself when necessary to bring your prophecy

Suzette A. Fox

into fruition. Too many people often give up too quickly on
what God has prophesied over them and are deceived by the
enemy into thinking that their prophecy was a lie. As a
result, they never believe another prophecy or another
prophet. There are false prophets, but with discernment from
the Holy Spirit, God will pinpoint the ones that are false.
Always keep your prophecy on the wall of prayer.

MEDITATE:

For we wrestle not against flesh and blood, but against
principalities, against powers, against the rulers of the
darkness of this world, against spiritual wickedness in high
places. Ephesians 6:12

Then thine handmaid said, The word of my lord the king
shall now be comfortable: for as an angel of God, so *is* my
lord the king to discern good and bad: therefore the Lord thy
God will be with thee. 2 Samuel 14:17

For he shall give his angels charge over thee, to keep thee in
all thy ways. Psalm 91:11

REFLECTION

Take some time to reflect on today's devotion.

Reflecting on today's devotion, is there any prophecy you've received that you believe is being held up?

_____

_____

_____

_____

If yes, have you given up on them?

_____

_____

_____

_____

Whether your answer is yes or no, stay focused on manifesting them or refocus your attention and stand on the promises of God.

List the prophetic words you have received and wait to hear from God. He will always remind you of what has been prophesied over you and align it through His word. Journal what the Lord speaks to you of your forth-telling (stating the present, declaration, truth) and flow with His direction regarding your foretelling (future). Don't lose focus. I can assure you as you keep in alignment with God you will see those prophecies come to pass.

_____

_____

_____

_____

_____

_____

_____

_____

NO ONE LEFT BEHIND

Now that you have a better understanding on why it is important to war over your prophecy, take this opportunity to encourage and teach someone else what you have learned.

_____

_____

_____

_____

_____

_____

_____

_____

_____

For I know the thoughts that I think toward you, saith the Lord, thoughts of peace, and not of evil, to give you an expected end.
Jeremiah 29:11

JOURNAL YOUR DAY

Suzette A. Fox

_____
_____
_____
_____
_____
_____
_____
_____
_____
_____
_____
_____
_____
_____
_____
_____
_____
_____
_____
_____
_____
_____
_____
_____

This charge I commit unto thee, son Timothy, according to the prophecies which went before on thee, that thou by them mightest war a good warfare
1 Timothy 1:18

15

DRINK FROM THE WELL

Once we have an encounter with God, we will never thirst again. The word of God and the Holy Ghost are our well, and we are allowed to eat and drink from it daily. Drinking from the well rejuvenates and strengthens our spirit man, changes our soulish desires to God desire and makes our heart a heart of flesh so that God can reshape us for His purpose and glory. The refreshing that we receive from God's well of living water saturates our mind to have a mind of Christ. I once walked away from God because I felt He was taking too long to answer my prayer. I said to God, "I am going to do me." And so, I did. I went back to the clubs, but the clubs did not want me. The Holy Ghost that resided in me felt very out of place, and I didn't even know what to do in the club. I would just sit there. My family would ask if I was ok or why did I come to the club to just sit. But, little did they or myself know that when you drink from the well and become saturated with the living water, it's very hard to get to a completely dry place. Especially when God has His warriors, His watchmen on the wall, calling your name in prayer reminding Him of His promises. When I walked away from God, I stayed away from the Lord for about three years. I know that prayers were going up on my behalf for my soul, because no matter what I did out there, it just did not feel right. Finally, God arrested me, and I returned to His kingdom. I submitted to the call and allowed God to clean me up once again, drinking from the well that never runs dry. When we are outside of God's care and provision it is very dry, there is no hope and no peace. We aren't able to experience authentic love, and our lives are full of destruction. But when we are in fellowship with God there is hope, unconditional love and peace—everything we will ever need pertaining to life and godliness. Even when we are walking with Him, but it feels like we're in a dry place and we think God is not working, He is. He is just teaching us patience and how to have intimacy with Him in the midst of those dry patches.

MEDITATE:

But whosoever drinketh of the water that I shall give him shall never thirst; but the water that I shall give him shall be in him a well of water springing up into everlasting life. John 4:14

So two *or* three cities wandered unto one city, to drink water; but they were not satisfied: yet have ye not returned unto me, saith the Lord. Amos 4:8

O Lord, the hope of Israel, all that forsake thee shall be ashamed, *and* they that depart from me shall be written in the earth, because they have forsaken the Lord, the fountain of living waters. Jeremiah 17:13

REFLECTION

Take some time to reflect on today's devotion.

As you reflect on today's devotion, what emotions do you feel?

_____

_____

_____

_____

Are you becoming rejuvenated spiritually?

_____

_____

_____

_____

If yes, write your thoughts on your observation. Also, how can you continue drinking from the well?

_____

_____

_____

_____

If no, write your thoughts on your observation. What do you think would inspire you to reconnect and stay connected?

_____

_____

_____

I encourage you to continue in God's word and prayer. Do not become discouraged but press towards the mark. God's desire is for you to drink from His well that will never run dry.

NO ONE LEFT BEHIND

Now that you have been drinking from the well that's keeping you spiritually connected, how can you teach and assist someone else?

_____

_____

_____

_____

_____

_____

_____

_____

_____

_____

He that believeth on me, as the scripture hath said, out of his belly shall flow rivers of living water.   John 7:38

Suzette A. Fox

JOURNAL YOUR DAY

_____
_____
_____
_____
_____
_____
_____
_____
_____
_____
_____
_____
_____
_____
_____
_____
_____
_____
_____
_____
_____
_____
_____
_____
_____

93

Jesus answered and said unto her, Whosoever drinketh of this water shall thirst again.   John 4:13

16

SERVE THE LORD WITH
A THANKFUL HEART

"Rejoice in the Lord alway: and again I say, Rejoice" (Philippians 4:4). No matter your circumstances, trust God with a thankful heart because we can see God's glory in His love, protection and provision for us. Many times, trying circumstances are allowed in our lives to bring us closer to God so we should never despise the things we go through in life. As God took me through my purging process, I had a season where I didn't have much money, but it was very important for us to celebrate birthdays in our home. I wasn't in a place to celebrate my son's birthday like I would have liked to, but I was thankful for his life. I thanked God that he is a healthy, handsome young man with a great personality who is excelling in school and loving the Lord. I explained to him that even though we were not able to celebrate like we used to, I thanked God for giving him another year to accomplish great things. He understood and thanked God himself for another year of a great life. He has an abundance of love and joy in the Lord; therefore, he was not looking for material things. He was thankful for God being in his life. God always looks at our response no matter where we are or what we have experienced in life. Even if we do not get our heart's desire in the time frame we want it or if we don't get what we desire at all, He is looking at how we posture our hearts toward Him. When we're going through tough times, would we still love on Him or turn away from Him as though He owes us something. Are we going to complain and reminisce about our Egypt experience as though it was better than what we now have with God? Or are we going to stand on God's word, in faith, knowing that whatever His word says, it will come to pass? God never looks at our need, He always looks at our faith, because He is a faithful Father. He is continuously taking care of His children. We should always come before the Lord with thanksgiving, never come before Him grudgingly. His word says to be content in any state that we are in. Keep in mind, He will never leave us in a low state, but our faith will show His glory and get us out of that place and into His best for us. He is a good Father!

MEDITATE:

O give thanks unto the Lord; for *he is* good; for his mercy *endureth* for ever.   1 Chronicles 16:34

In everything give thanks: for this is the will of God in Christ Jesus concerning you.   1 Thessalonians 5:18

And let the peace of God rule in your hearts, to the which also ye are called in one body; and be ye thankful. Colossians 3:15

And whatsoever ye do in word or deed, do all in the name of the Lord Jesus, giving thanks to God and the Father by him. Colossians 3:17

Continue in prayer, and watch in the same with thanksgiving. Colossians 4:2

REFLECTION

Take some time to reflect on today's devotion.

As you look back at diverse circumstances, did you approach God with a thankful heart or a grudging heart?

_____

_____

_____

_____

From today's devotion what will be your approach when circumstances are beyond your control?

_____

_____

_____

_____

As you reflect on your circumstances, write down those that are both good and bad to see what God may be teaching you in those areas.

_____

_____

_____

_____

_____

_____

_____

Suzette A. Fox

NO ONE LEFT BEHIND

Now that you understand the importance of being thankful no matter your circumstances, think on ways you can teach and help others to learn this valued principle.

_____
_____
_____
_____
_____
_____
_____
_____
_____
_____
_____
_____
_____
_____
_____
_____
_____
_____
_____

And let the peace of God rule in your hearts, to the which also ye are called in one body; and be ye thankful.
Colossians 3:15

Suzette A. Fox

JOURNAL YOUR DAY

_____

_____

_____

_____

_____

_____

_____

_____

_____

_____

_____

_____

_____

_____

_____

_____

_____

_____

_____

_____

_____

_____

_____

_____

_____

_____

Suzette A. Fox

_____
_____
_____
_____
_____
_____
_____
_____
_____
_____
_____
_____
_____
_____
_____
_____
_____
_____
_____
_____
_____
_____
_____
_____
_____

O give thanks unto the Lord; for *he is* good; for his mercy *endureth* for ever.
1 Chronicles 16:34

17

PURPOSE OF FASTING

I have found that when God calls me on a fast, it is not for my personal gain, but God's gain or benefit in me. God often calls us to a fast to rest in Him, so that our spirit man can grow. Fasting is beneficial spiritually and physically. As God strengthens our spirit man, He is also strengthening our natural man. When we fast, it is imperative that we focus on God, reading His word and staying in worship. Fasting is a sacrifice that draws us closer to God. It is not to be used as an opportunity to boast to others about what you're doing as the Pharisees did. Isaiah 58, in *The Message* translation, gives us the full purpose of why we fast as God leads us. Verses 3–14 tells us, "Well, here's why: The bottom line on your 'fast days' is profit. You drive your employees much too hard. You fast, but at the same time you bicker and fight. You fast, but you swing a mean fist. The kind of fasting you do won't get your prayers off the ground. Do you think this is the kind of fast day I'm after: a day to show off humility? To put on a pious long face and parade around solemnly in black? Do you call that fasting, a fast day that I, God, would like? This is the kind of fast day I'm after: to break the chains of injustice, get rid of exploitation in the workplace, free the oppressed, cancel debts. What I'm interested in seeing you do is: sharing your food with the hungry, inviting the homeless poor into your homes putting clothes on the shivering ill-clad, being available to your own families. Do this and the lights will turn on, and your lives will turn around at once. Your righteousness will pave your way. The God of glory will secure your passage. Then when you pray, God will answer. You'll call out for help and I'll say, 'Here I am.' If you get rid of unfair practices, quit blaming victims, quit gossiping about other people's sins, If you are generous with the hungry and start giving yourselves to the down-and-out, Your lives will begin to glow in the darkness, your shadowed lives will be bathed in sunlight. I will always show you where to go. I'll give you a full life in the emptiest of places–firm muscles, strong bones. You'll be like a well-watered garden, a gurgling spring that never runs dry. You'll use the old rubble of past lives to build a new, rebuild the foundations from out of your past. You'll be known as those who can fix anything, restore old ruins, rebuild and renovate, make the community livable again enjoy God! Oh, I'll make you ride high and soar above it all. I'll make you feast on the inheritance of your ancestor Jacob.' Yes! God says so!"

Suzette A. Fox

MEDITATE:

But thou, when thou fastest, anoint thine head, and wash thy face; 18) That thou appear not unto men to fast, but unto thy Father which is in secret: and thy Father, which seeth in secret, shall reward thee openly. Matthew 6:17-18

Therefore also now, saith the Lord, turn ye *even* to me with all your heart, and with fasting, and with weeping, and with mourning: And rend your heart, and not your garments, and turn unto the Lord your God: for he *is* gracious and merciful, slow to anger, and of great kindness, and repenteth him of the evil. Joel 2:12-13

So we fasted and besought our God of this: and he was intreated of us. Ezra 8:23

_x000D_

_x000D_

Suzette A. Fox

REFLECTION

Take some time to reflect on today's devotion.

Did today's devotion clarify your purpose for fasting and who should call the fast?

_____

_____

_____

_____

_____

Prior to today, did you fast according to what the scripture states above?

_____

_____

_____

_____

_____

_____

_____

If yes, continue to always allow God to call you on a fast and adhere to His direction.

If no, I pray that today's devotion encourages and enlightens you on the importance of allowing God to call your fast.

105

Suzette A. Fox

No one left behind

Now that you have clarification and confirmation on the importance of allowing God to call a fast, how will you teach and enlighten someone else about what you have learned?

_____

_____

_____

_____

_____

_____

_____

_____

_____

_____

_____

_____

_____

_____

_____

_____

Is not this the fast that I have chosen? to loose the bands of wickedness, to undo
the heavy burdens, and to let the oppressed go free, and that ye break every yoke?
Isaiah 58:6

JOURNAL YOUR DAY

Suzette A. Fox

_____

_____

_____

_____

_____

_____

_____

_____

_____

_____

_____

_____

_____

_____

_____

_____

_____

_____

_____

_____

_____

And it came to pass, when I heard these words, that I sat down and wept, and
mourned *certain* days, and fasted, and prayed before the God of heaven.
Nehemiah 1:4

18

PRAY FOR OUR LEADERS

It's imperative to cover our leaders, spiritual and secular in our prayers. God chose them for such a time, even when we may not understand their direction or actions. Prayer is the perfect time to seek God's face with your concerns, rather than to speaking to others about God's leaders. Whether they are spiritual or secular leaders, God has chosen them to do His will, we did not choose them. One man or woman will never be able to please everyone, but if God place us under their leadership, it's imperative to cover them in prayer. The enemy is always looking for ways to discredit our leaders, especially our spiritual leaders. They will have their flaws. They may not be perfect, but when God shows us imperfections, it's our responsibility to cover them. It is not the time to talk about them to others, but the time to pray that God would open their eyes, ears and soften their hearts to hear from Him and respond to His direction. All God desires is for us to honor our leaders and we can do that through praying His perfect will over their lives. Our leaders have a very heavy mantle to carry to lead God's people. Look at Moses during the Exodus. The people complained while at the same time they were saying, "Yes, Lord." The problem was that their response was from their lips and not their heart. Their actions show that they never had an authentic relationship with God. God desires for His people

Suzette A. Fox

to worship Him at the foot of the mount when He comes into our presence and not become fearful. When we spend time in prayer for our leaders, it will give them the opportunity to go up to the top of the mountain and spend time with God to bring direction back to us. Help lift up your leaders, and don't tear them down.

Side note: Read the book of Exodus to understand both the role of a leader and his followers.

MEDITATE:

Scriptures to Pray for our leaders:

For wisdom: But the wisdom that is from above is first pure, then peaceable, gentle, *and* easy to be intreated, full of mercy and good fruits, without partiality, and without hypocrisy. James 3:17

For a pure heart: Finally, brethren, whatsoever things are true, whatsoever things are honest, whatsoever things *are* just, whatsoever things *are* pure, whatsoever things *are* lovely, whatsoever things *are* of good report; if *there be* any virtue, and if *there be* any praise, think on these things. Philippians 4:8

For gentleness: And the servant of the Lord must not strive; but be gentle unto all *men*, apt to teach, patient, In meekness instructing those that oppose themselves; if God peradventure will give them repentance to the acknowledging of the truth. 2 Timothy 2:24–25

For sincerity: For we are not as many, which corrupt the word of God: but as of sincerity, but as of God, in the sight of God speak we in Christ. 2 Corinthians 2:17

REFLECTION

Take some time reflect on today's devotion.

What are your thoughts regarding the importance of covering our leaders?

_____

_____

_____

_____

_____

Do you believe that God has called only a certain group or all of us to cover our leaders in prayer?

_____

_____

_____

_____

_____

_____

God has called all of us to pray for our leaders, but He will certainly align us according to whom He desires us to target in prayer. It is imperative to be sensitive to the Holy Spirit and hear what the Lord is saying about that leader (or leaders) in order to cover accordingly.

List the leaders and areas of their lives that God has called you to cover. Also find scriptures to pray over them.

_____

_____

_____

_____

_____

_____

_____

_____

No one left behind

List ways that you will teach and advocate to others the importance in covering our leaders in prayer.

_____

_____

_____

_____

_____

_____

_____

_____

_____

_____

Let nothing be done through strife or vainglory; but in lowliness of mind let each esteem other better than themselves.
Philippians 2:3

Journal Your Day

_____
_____
_____
_____
_____
_____
_____
_____
_____
_____
_____
_____
_____
_____
_____
_____
_____
_____
_____
_____
_____
_____
_____
_____
_____

Suzette A. Fox

I exhort therefore, that, first of all, supplications, prayers, intercessions, and giving of thanks, be made for all men; For kings, and for all that are in authority; that we may lead a quiet and peaceable life in all godliness and honesty.

1 Timothy 2:1-2

19

THE HOLY SPIRIT

The prophet Joel prophesied about the Holy Spirit in Joel 2:28, "And it shall come to pass afterward, *that* I will pour out my Spirit upon all flesh; and your sons and your daughters shall prophesy, your old men shall dream dreams, your young men shall see visions." This prophecy was manifested on the day of Pentecost, "And when the day of Pentecost was fully come, they were all with one accord in one place. And suddenly there came a sound from heaven as of a rushing mighty wind, and it filled all the house where they were sitting. And there appeared unto them cloven tongues like as of fire, and it sat upon each of them. And they were all filled with the Holy Ghost, and began to speak with other tongues, as the Spirit gave them utterance" (Acts 2:1-4). Peter went on to explain what was said by the prophet Joel to the people who thought the disciples were drunk in Acts 2:16-18. They were all on one accord, in unity, harmonious and in obedience to Jesus which is a key factor in all that we do. He told them to wait for the promise, and suddenly there came the infilling of the Holy Ghost. The Holy Ghost is our guide, our comforter, our healer, our encourager, our counselor, and our strength. Jesus also said to the disciples in Acts 1:8, "But ye shall receive power, after that the Holy Ghost is come upon you: and ye shall be witnesses unto me both in Jerusalem, and in all Judaea, and in Samaria, and unto the uttermost part of the earth." Jesus said that the power that we receive from the infilling of the Holy Ghost will cause us to do greater works than He did. In John 14:12, He said, "Verily, verily, I say unto you, He that believeth on me, the works that I do shall he do also; and greater *works* than these shall he do; because I go unto my Father." The Holy Spirit will transform us by the renewing of our mind from sinner to saint. He, in turn, can use us as holy vessels to work through to reach lives throughout the nations.

MEDITATE:

And I will put my spirit within you, and cause you to walk in my statutes, and ye shall keep my judgments, and do *them*. Ezekiel 36:27

Even the Spirit of truth; whom the world cannot receive, because it seeth him not, neither knoweth him: but ye know him; for he dwelleth with you, and shall be in you. John 14:17

Now the Lord is that Spirit: and where the Spirit of the Lord is, there is liberty. 2 Corinthians 3:17

But the Comforter, which is the Holy Ghost, whom the Father will send in my name, he shall teach you all things, and bring all things to your remembrance, whatsoever I have said unto you. John 14:26

REFLECTION

Take some time to reflect on today's devotion.

As you reflect on today's devotion, what are your thoughts regarding being filled with the Holy Ghost to do the "greater works"?

_____

_____

_____

Do you have the infilling of the Holy Ghost according to Acts 2:38?

_____

_____

If no, I encourage you to continue seeking our heavenly Father in prayer as you wait on the gift.

If yes, continue to allow the Holy Ghost to have preeminence in your daily walk with Him. Let the Spirit of God refresh you with the Holy Spirit often.

What in this devotion stood out to you?

_____

_____

_____

_____

Suzette A. Fox

How can it impact your daily walk with God?

_____

_____

_____

_____

NO ONE LEFT BEHIND
Now that you have embraced the importance of having the infilling of the Holy Ghost, how can you teach and encourage someone who has the gift but are not confident of its importance in their daily lives? Also, how would you encourage someone who does not have the gift?

_____

_____

_____

_____

_____

_____

_____

_____

_____

_____

_____

But ye are not in the flesh, but in the Spirit, if so be that the Spirit of God dwell in
you. Now if any man have not the Spirit of Christ, he is none of his.
Romans 8:9

JOURNAL YOUR DAY

_____
_____
_____
_____
_____
_____
_____
_____
_____
_____
_____
_____
_____
_____
_____
_____
_____
_____
_____
_____
_____
_____
_____
_____
_____
_____

Suzette A. Fox

_____
_____
_____
_____
_____
_____
_____
_____
_____
_____
_____
_____
_____
_____
_____
_____
_____
_____
_____
_____
_____
_____
_____
_____

And I will pray the Father, and he shall give you another Comforter, that he may
abide with you forever.
John 14:16

20

WORSHIP = INTIMACY

Worship shows reverence and adoration to God. I love to worship because it brings me into such an intimate place with God. Intimacy is a state of having a personal and private relationship with someone. Our soul desires intimacy, and if we are not careful we can be intimate with the wrong people. We can also find ourselves worshipping someone or something more than we worship God. Worshipping God reminds us that God is the authentic lover of our soul and we find ourselves overshadowed by an abundance of peace and joy when we become intimate with Him. During times of turmoil and uncertainty not knowing what to do or how to make sense of confusing and distressing situations, worshipping God brings His presence into that very situation. In His presence is clarity, peace and joy that will ultimately give you the strength to stand strong as a soldier and not allow your circumstance to sway or bend you into submission. When you worship the joy of the Lord becomes your strength. We are face-to-face with God just as Moses experienced on the mountaintop in Exodus, chapter 20. Worship changes our mindset and sanctifies our hearts to be set apart to the likeness and image of God. It's a transformation just as a caterpillar transforms into a butterfly. We must worship from our hearts and not just our lips. The heart is the central organ in our body which pumps

Suzette A. Fox

blood to help our other organs function accordingly. In parallel comparison, worship is the spiritual blood that pumps into our spirit or heart which will then align our mind body and soul to be pleasing to God. We must worship God in spirit and in truth as stated in John 4:23. "But the hour cometh, and now is, when the true worshippers shall worship the Father in spirit and in truth: for the Father seeketh such to worship him." Obedience, trusting in God, humility, serving, unconditional love, operating in the fruit of the Spirit (Galatians 5:22–23)—all of these are forms of worship. To worship God in spirit and truth necessarily involves loving Him with your whole heart and allowing Him to be your everything.

MEDITATE:

Give unto the Lord the glory due unto his name; worship the Lord in the beauty of holiness.   Psalm 29:2

O come, let us worship and bow down: let us kneel before the Lord our maker.   Psalm 95:6

O Lord, thou art my God; I will exalt thee, I will praise thy name; for thou hast done wonderful things; thy counsels of old are faithfulness and truth. Isaiah 25:1

God is a Spirit: and they that worship him must worship him in spirit and in truth. John 4:24

Bless the Lord, O my soul: and all that is within me, bless his holy name. Psalm 103:1

O God, thou art my God; early will I seek thee: my soul thirsteth for thee, my flesh longeth for thee in a dry and thirsty land, where no water is. Psalm 63:1

Suzette A. Fox

REFLECTION

Take some time to reflect on today's devotion.

What are your thoughts on worship and its importance in the life of a believer?

_____

_____

_____

_____

Is there any person, place or thing you have a tendency of worshipping? Be very honest with yourself, it's just you and God in this moment.

_____

_____

_____

_____

If yes, bring those things listed before our heavenly Father in prayer, so that they can become less important and worshipping God becomes more important.

If no, I encourage you to stay focused and not allow anyone or anything to take that place of worshipping our heavenly Father.

Reminisce on some of your intimate moments with the Father. Keep those moments alive.

_____

_____

_____

_____

_____

_____

_____

_____

NO ONE LEFT BEHIND

Now that you have embraced the importance of worship, how can you teach and encourage someone else to do the same?

_____

_____

_____

_____

_____

_____

_____

_____

_____

_____

Exalt ye the Lord our God, and worship at his footstool; *for* he *is* holy.
Psalm 99:5

Journal Your Day

Suzette A. Fox

_____
_____
_____
_____
_____
_____
_____
_____
_____
_____
_____
_____
_____
_____
_____
_____
_____
_____
_____
_____
_____
_____
_____
_____

Saying with a loud voice, Fear God, and give glory to him; for the hour of his judgment is come: and worship him that made heaven, and earth, and the sea, and the fountains of waters.

Revelations 14:7

21

GOD WILL HEAL THE
BROKEN HEARTED

"He healeth the broken in heart, and bindeth up their wounds" (Psalm 147:3). God is always true to His word. We all have been hurt many times in our lives and may have never understood why. The violator may not have realized they hurt you or the pain they may have caused you as well because they are also victims of a broken heart. As the old adage goes, "Hurt people hurt people." When a person has a broken spirit and doesn't know how to overcome the pain they have experienced at the hand of another person, it becomes a vicious cycle. How does someone heal from a broken heart? Acknowledging that you are broken and hurting from your brokenness, and desiring help is the first step. Prayer is the ultimate place to start. God is a loving Father who can heal and erase all traces, whether physical or verbal, of the scars, fears and anxiety that may have crippled you. God can and will heal your broken heart. The situation may be so painful that you may also need to seek godly professional help, but don't allow shame to make you feel as though you're not trusting in God. There is nothing to be ashamed of; God knows all about what you've gone through. I have learned through my training as a chaplain, that if we do not face and acknowledge past hurts, we are only putting a bandage on it then moving on with life, or so we think. However, there will come a time where we will break, because of another situation resting on that scar like salt. It is imperative to face those hurts with God and godly professional help to ensure that there is no trace of it remains in your life or memory. We also have to be able to forgive and make right by someone if we have deliberately or accidentally caused hurt or pain to anyone. By doing so, we won't become a repetitive violator. Remember, we forgive and are forgiven by the love of our heavenly Father. The Bible says in 1 Peter 5:7, "Casting all your care upon him; for he careth for you." It also says, "The Lord is nigh unto them that are of a broken heart; and saveth such as be of a contrite spirit. Many are the afflictions of the righteous: but the Lord delivereth him out of them all" (Psalm 34:18-19). God is our Deliverer.

MEDITATE:

I can do all things through Christ which strengtheneth me.
Philippians 4:13

Yea, though I walk through the valley of the shadow of
death, I will fear no evil: for thou *art* with me; thy rod and
thy staff they comfort me. Psalm 23:4

Peace I leave with you, my peace I give unto you: not as the
world giveth, give I unto you. Let not your heart be troubled,
neither let it be afraid. John 14:27

Cast thy burden upon the LORD, and he shall sustain thee:
he shall never suffer the righteous to be moved. Psalm 55:22

He healeth the broken in heart, and bindeth up their wounds.
Psalm 147:3

REFLECTION

Take some time to reflect on today's devotion.

After reading today's devotion, how do you feel emotionally?

_____

_____

_____

_____

_____

Did today's devotion bring back any past hurts that have not been dealt with?

_____

_____

_____

_____

_____

If yes, list those past hurts. Be very honest with yourself, this is your time with God for healing.

_____

_____

_____

_____

_____

Suzette A. Fox

If no, I encourage you, while in prayer, to always ask our heavenly Father to bring to your attention of any deep hidden hurts in your heart (all of those things you never knew were there).

NO ONE LEFT BEHIND
Now that you have embraced the importance of confronting your hurts and brokenness, how can you teach and encourage someone else to do the same?

_____
_____
_____
_____
_____
_____
_____
_____
_____
_____
_____
_____

My flesh and my heart faileth: *but* God *is* the strength of my heart, and my portion for ever.   Psalm 73:26

JOURNAL YOUR DAY

_____
_____
_____
_____
_____
_____
_____
_____
_____
_____
_____
_____
_____
_____
_____
_____
_____
_____
_____
_____
_____
_____
_____
_____
_____

Suzette A. Fox

_____
_____
_____
_____
_____
_____
_____
_____
_____
_____
_____
_____
_____
_____
_____
_____
_____
_____
_____
_____
_____
_____
_____
_____
_____

For I reckon that the sufferings of this present time *are* not worthy *to be compared*
with the glory which shall be revealed in us.
Romans 8:18

22

LOYALTY TO GOD

Loyalty or loyal is defined in *Merriam-Webster's Dictionary* as "unswerving in allegiance; faithful in allegiance to one's lawful sovereign or government." Are we loyal to God because of the blessing or is it because of who He is? In my early walk with God, I thought that once I became born again, baptized in Jesus Name, filled with the Holy Ghost and living for God according to His word, I assumed that I would not have any more problem in my life. My loyalty to God revolved around Him blessing me, so I was not entirely loyal to Him. My loyalty was conditional; It was based on me getting the blessing. After growing in my relationship with God over the years, I learned that this is not the reason Jesus went to the cross for my sin, and not the reason God created me in His image and likeness. God desires to fellowship with us. The blessing is a benefit of having the relationship. After we get to know Him, He shows us all He's given us such as "dominion over the fishes of the sea, the fowl of the air, over the cattle, and over all the earth and over every creeping thing that creepeth upon the earth" (Genesis 1:26). That's a bonus to being loyal to God. Remember, "he is a rewarder of them that diligently seek him" (Hebrews 11:6). God wants our lives, the stuff we seek comes when we seek Him first as our heavenly Father (see Matthew 6:33). He wants us to faithfully love, honor, and worship Him seeking His face about every aspect of our life. When we are loyal to God, it will enable us to be loyal to those whom He has given authority over us. It will cause us to die to yourself. The disciples are a great example of showing their loyalty to Jesus when they left all of their riches and followed Him. Other biblical examples are Elisha's loyalty to Elijah, David to Saul and Jonathan to David. When Elijah rested his mantle on Elisha, he left his family and sat under Elijah so that he could mentor him. David was loyal to Saul even when Saul desired to kill him. Jonathan's father even desired to kill David but that did not sway Jonathan even from continuing his loyalty to David to teach him the ways of the palace. God is always looking for those who are loyal to Him. Second Chronicles 16:9 says, "For the eyes of the Lord run to and fro throughout the whole earth, to shew himself strong in the behalf of *them* whose heart *is* perfect toward Him."

Suzette A. Fox

MEDITATE:

My son, fear thou the Lord and the king: *and* meddle not with them that are given to change. Proverbs 24:21

I *counsel thee* to keep the king's commandment, and *that* in regard of the oath of God. Ecclesiastes 8:2

Know therefore that the LORD thy God, he is God, the faithful God, which keepeth covenant and mercy with them that love him and keep his commandments to a thousand generations. Deuteronomy 7:9

And he said, LORD God of Israel, there is no God like thee, in heaven above, or on earth beneath, who keepest covenant and mercy with thy servants that walk before thee with all their heart. 1 Kings 8:23

And said, O LORD God of Israel, there is no God like thee in the heaven, nor in the earth; which keepest covenant, and shewest mercy unto thy servants, that walk before thee with all their hearts. 2 Chronicles 6:14

Suzette A. Fox

REFLECTION

Take some time to reflect on today's devotion.

What are your thoughts on being loyal to God?

_____

_____

_____

_____

_____

What are your thoughts on being loyal to others?

_____

_____

_____

_____

Does it line up with the word of God?

_____

_____

_____

_____

_____

If yes, I encourage you to continue to allow the word of God to help you stay in alignment with your loyalty to God and to others even when people are not loyal to you.

140

Suzette A. Fox

If no, I encourage you to continue seeking our heavenly Father in prayer to teach you through His word how to be loyal to Him and especially to others even when they are not loyal to you.

NO ONE LEFT BEHIND

Now that you have embrace the importance of loyalty to God and to others, how can you demonstrate its importance to others?

_____

_____

_____

_____

_____

_____

_____

_____

_____

_____

_____

_____

_____

_____

They say unto him, Caesar's. Then saith he unto them, Render therefore unto Caesar the things which are Caesar's; and unto God the things that are God's.
Matthew 22:21

JOURNAL YOUR DAY

_____

_____

_____

_____

_____

_____

_____

_____

_____

_____

_____

_____

_____

_____

_____

_____

_____

_____

_____

_____

_____

_____

_____

_____

Suzette A. Fox

_____

_____

_____

_____

_____

_____

_____

_____

_____

_____

_____

_____

_____

_____

_____

_____

_____

_____

_____

_____

_____

_____

Now therefore, if ye will obey my voice indeed, and keep my covenant, then ye shall
be a peculiar treasure unto me above all people: for all the earth *is* mine.
Exodus 19:5

Suzette A. Fox

23

YOUR VISION

Vision is defined on *Dictionary.com* as "an experience in which a personage, thing, or event appears vividly or credibly to the mind, although not actually present, often under a divine influence." What is the vision God has given you to execute here on earth? Is your vision sitting dormant because of fear, doubt or lack of confidence? I challenge you to allow God to order your steps to execute the vision that He has given you. I never knew my purpose or at least did not pay attention to the details of God's divine purpose for my life because I was too busy creating my own. After walking with God for many years, I began to desire to be in full alignment with God's plan for my life. Our vision is imparted from God according to where we are in our relationship with Him. If you desire to be the god of your life and not allow Jehovah God to be your Lord, then you will certainly miss His divine vision and plan for your life. This is where I was. When God showed me the call on my life and gave me His vision for His business and ministry, I felt unworthy. I believed I did not have the ability nor the resources to do what He called me to do. Nevertheless, I continue to flow with God and trust Him in the process. Every aspect of His vision is according to His timing to execute the step-by-step plan to birth His baby. He did not miss a beat. God connected me with the right people from

144

the beginning to the end. I did not flow with my agenda, I did not lose focus, even while being stretched by my mentors and coach. When payments were due for particular assignments, God made sure the money was there. He even taught me how to be articulate when negotiating deals. When God gives a vision, He will always give provision. When you begin to execute your vision by being obedient and stepping out on faith, God divinely connects you with the people, places and things you need to fulfill that vision. As I ride the wave of His vision for my life, settling and accepting it, I know that God is with me, ordering my steps. I am becoming more confident and excited about the end result with each step that I take. It's an honor to be the earthen vessel chosen by God to execute His work. Keep in mind our vision is to empower our lives and the lives of others which is in itself a rewarding experience.

Suzette A. Fox

MEDITATE:

Where *there is* no vision, the people perish: but he that keepeth the law, happy *is* he. Proverbs 29:18

After these things the word of the Lord came unto Abram in a vision, saying, Fear not, Abram: I *am* thy shield, *and* thy exceeding great reward. Genesis 15:1

And he said, Hear now my words: If there be a prophet among you, I the LORD will make myself known unto him in a vision, and will speak unto him in a dream.
Numbers 12:6

Be not ye therefore like unto them: for your father knoweth what things ye have need of, before ye ask him. Matthew 6:8

The LORD openeth the eyes of the blind: the LORD raiseth them that are bowed down: the LORD loveth the righteous. Psalm 146:8

REFLECTION

Take some time to reflect on today's devotion.

What are your thoughts on receiving God's divine vision for your life?

_____

_____

_____

Have you stifled the vision given to you by our heavenly Father?

_____

_____

_____

_____

_____

If yes, list the visions God has shown you and take it to our Father in faith and with prayer for direction and the wisdom to fulfill it. Be obedient to do what He tells you to do.

_____

_____

_____

_____

_____

_____

If no, I encourage you to focus on God and as He leads and directs you, listen to His voice obediently to fulfill His vision for your life.

NO ONE LEFT BEHIND

Now that you understand that God's vision for your life is better and more fulfilling than anything you could ever dream for yourself, how can you encourage someone else to trust God during the process of executing their vision from Him?

_____
_____
_____
_____
_____
_____
_____
_____
_____
_____

And God spake unto Israel in the visions of the night, and said, Jacob, Jacob. And he said, Here *am* I. And he said, I *am* God, the God of thy father: fear not to go down into Egypt; for I will there make of thee a great nation: I will go down with thee into Egypt; and I will also surely bring thee up *again*: and Joseph shall put his hand upon thine eyes. Genesis 46:2-4

Suzette A. Fox

JOURNAL YOUR DAY

_____
_____
_____
_____
_____
_____
_____
_____
_____
_____
_____
_____
_____
_____
_____
_____
_____
_____
_____
_____
_____
_____
_____
_____

Suzette A. Fox

_____
_____
_____
_____
_____
_____
_____
_____
_____
_____
_____
_____
_____
_____
_____
_____
_____
_____
_____
_____
_____
_____
_____
_____
_____

Where *there is* no vision, the people perish: but he that keepeth the law, happy *is* he.   Proverbs 29:18

24

GOD'S GRACE

Grace is defined by *Merriam-Webster's Dictionary* as "unmerited divine assistance given to humans for their sanctification or set apart virtue coming from God's special favor." We can use grace in so many areas of our lives. We bless our food or say grace before meals, we have a grace period to pay our bills, and God has given us the grace to execute His will on earth. As God continued to prepare me for His ministry and the marketplace, He said work only five hours per day and the rest of my time I would spend with Him. In your natural mind, that may seem absurd, but God said He would give me the grace to do so. However, when you know you're in alignment with God and in obedience, His grace will be sufficient to do what He has called you to do. When I was being prepared for His purpose, in that secret place in God, He handled everything that would be a distraction to me. From bills not being paid late, to no insufficient fund charges in my account—He supplied all my needs. I did not need to borrow because I made my requests known to God and He is my great provider. In Psalm 24:1 it says, "The earth *is* the Lord's, and the fulness thereof; the world, and they that dwell therein." There is nothing to worry about when you're flowing in God's grace. Paul made it known that no matter his circumstance, as long as he's in the will of God, God's grace was sufficient for him. Second Corinthians 12:7–9 recounts what Paul said, "And lest I should be exalted above measure through the abundance of the revelations, there was given to me a thorn in the flesh, the messenger of Satan to buffet me, lest I should be exalted above measure. For this thing I besought the Lord thrice, that it might depart from me. And he said unto me, My grace is sufficient for thee: for my strength is made perfect in weakness. Most gladly therefore will I rather glory in my infirmities, that the power of Christ may rest upon me." I could not have done this in my strength nor with my intellect. I serve a God who is alive, true and faithful to His word—He is all-powerful and perfect.

MEDITATE:

And Moses said unto the LORD, See, thou sayest unto me, Bring up this people: and thou hast not let me know whom thou wilt send with me. Yet thou hast said, I know thee by name, and thou hast also found grace in my sight. Exodus 33:12

For the LORD God *is* a sun and shield: the LORD will give grace and glory: no good *thing* will he withhold from them that walk uprightly. Psalm 84:11

And the Word was made flesh, and dwelt among us, (and we beheld his glory, the glory as of the only begotten of the Father,) full of grace and truth. John 1:14

But unto every one of us is given grace according to the measure of the gift of Christ. Ephesians 4:7

REFLECTION

Take some time to reflect on today's devotion.

As you reflect on today's devotion what are your thoughts on God's grace?

_____
_____
_____
_____
_____

How has God shown you grace in your life?

_____
_____
_____
_____
_____

As you reflect on the grace of God, write your adoration to your heavenly Father. (Whenever you revisit this page it will remind you of where you were then and where you are now).

_____
_____
_____
_____
_____

Suzette A. Fox

NO ONE LEFT BEHIND

Now that you have reflect on His grace race, how can you teach and encourage someone else that God's grace is sufficient?

_____

_____

_____

_____

_____

_____

_____

_____

_____

_____

_____

_____

_____

_____

_____

_____

_____

_____

_____

_____

And now for a little space grace hath been *shewed* from the LORD our God, to leave us a remnant to escape, and to give us a nail in his holy place, that our God may lighten our eyes, and give us a little reviving in our bondage.

Ezra 9:8

JOURNAL YOUR DAY

_____
_____
_____
_____
_____
_____
_____
_____
_____
_____
_____
_____
_____
_____
_____
_____
_____
_____
_____
_____
_____
_____
_____
_____
_____
_____

And Stephen, full of faith and power, did great wonders and miracles among the people.   Acts 6:8

25

OBEDIENCE

IS BETTER THAN SACRIFICE

OxfordDictionaries.com defines compliance as "with an order, request or law or submission to another's authority." When we are obedient, we are submitting to the authority of God's word and stepping out on faith. When we trust God's word wholeheartedly, we don't have to rely on anything else confirming what we believe. Obedience is also a form of worship. Those who worship God must worship Him "in spirit and in truth" (John 4:23). Worship is becoming intimate with God, and so in exercising that act of obedience, it carries the weight of sacrificing your will to the Father. Such as the case with Abraham in Genesis 22. When God directed Abraham to sacrifice his son that he loves dearly, on Mount Moriah. Abraham did not ask any questions. He gathered what he needed for the mission and he, along with his servants and son Isaac and went to Mount Moriah and God gave him instructions on what to do. Abraham's obedience allowed him to exercise his faith. To release your faith for something, you have to know who God is. After God gave Abraham the directions for the sacrifice, Abraham told his servant to wait while he and his son go to the mount to worship and that they would return afterward. How did Abraham know that he and his son would return?

Suzette A. Fox

Because Abraham knew His God and that God would provide an authentic sacrifice for the ceremony because of his obedience to step out in faith. In the end, God told Abraham that He would bless him and his seed in abundance and the number of them would be as counting the stars in heaven and the sand on the seashore. Now that's a lot of blessings because of obedience! Obedience unlocks many doors for our purpose of setting the captives free and healing the broken-hearted. God did not snatch us out of the enemy's camp to look cute, but to push us into our purpose which will then get us to our destiny. In my obeying God, I have had the opportunity to write many books and build a business and ministry with His direction. When we follow God's directives, we are releasing our control and giving Him control over our lives, but truthfully, I prefer God to have all the control! Once we release everything to Him, at least we know that we will be taken care of through an Abrahamic covenant. Through worship, obedience, and sacrifice you are giving up your will for God's will.

MEDITATE:

And he said unto them, Set your hearts unto all the words which I testify among you this day, which ye shall command your children to observe to do, all the words of this law. Deuteronomy 32:46

This book of the law shall not depart out of thy mouth; but thou shalt meditate therein day and night, that thou mayest observe to do according to all that is written therein: for then thou shalt make thy way prosperous, and then thou shalt have good success. Joshua 1:8

Not everyone that saith unto me, Lord, Lord, shall enter into the kingdom of heaven; but he that doeth the will of my Father which is in heaven. Matthew 7:21

And he answered and said unto them, My mother and my brethren are these which hear the word of God, and do it. Luke 8:21

REFLECTION

Take some time to reflect on today's devotion.

As you reflect, what are your thoughts on being obedient and its importance?

_____
_____
_____
_____

Have you ever struggled to obey? Write your thoughts, such as the emotion you felt and your physicality in that moment.

_____
_____
_____
_____
_____
_____
_____

How can you overcome any fear of obeying God's word wholeheartedly?

_____
_____
_____
_____
_____

Suzette A. Fox

No one left behind

Now that you have embraced the importance of obeying God wholeheartedly, how can you encourage someone in this area?

_____
_____
_____
_____
_____
_____
_____
_____
_____
_____
_____
_____
_____
_____
_____
_____
_____
_____
_____
_____

And he answered and said unto them, My mother and my brethren are these which hear the word of God, and do it.

Luke 8:21

JOURNAL YOUR DAY

Suzette A. Fox

_____
_____
_____
_____
_____
_____
_____
_____
_____
_____
_____
_____
_____
_____
_____
_____
_____
_____
_____
_____
_____
_____
_____
_____
_____

Therefore thou shalt love the Lord thy God, and keep his charge, and his statutes,
and his judgments, and his commandments, alway.
Deuteronomy 11:1

26

CULTIVATE YOUR GIFT

God, the great giver, has given each one of us a gift to walk in our vocation to execute His plan on earth. As stated in Acts 1:4, Jesus told the disciples to wait for the gift that the Father promised. In Acts 2, on the day of Pentecost, the disciples all received the gift being on one accord, then Peter gave instruction to the people who had gathered hearing the disciples speaking in their native language on how they too could receive the gift by repenting. The Holy Ghost is a gift promised to all of us, but we all also have a unique gift that the Holy Ghost works through. Ephesians 4:11 tells us about some of the gifts that flow in the different offices God gave to edify the Church according to a person's faith. Paul spoke of nine gifts in 1 Corinthians 12:8–11, "For to one is given by the Spirit the word of wisdom; to another the word of knowledge by the same Spirit; to another faith by the same Spirit; to another the gifts of healing by the same Spirit; to another the working of miracles; to another prophecy; to another discerning of spirits; to another *divers* kinds of tongues; to another the interpretation of tongues: But all these worketh that one and the selfsame Spirit, dividing to every man severally as he will." It is imperative to walk in our vocation as stated in Ephesians 4:1, "I therefore, the prisoner of the Lord, beseech you that ye walk worthy of the vocation wherewith ye are called." When we don't know our purpose, it can be frustrating because you can feel out of sync which sometimes leads to feeling worthless, inadequate, and a counterfeit. When you know your purpose, you strive to cultivate your gift to enhance your purpose. First Corinthians 12 provides a definitive understanding of the spiritual gifts given by God to edify the Body of Christ and how to cultivate and use them. After surrendering my will, God has been able to open my eyes to what my purpose is on earth. Walking in the plan of God will enhance your gift, your call, and your purpose and guide you to your destiny.

Suzette A. Fox

MEDITATE:

Humility: For I say, through the grace given unto me, to every man that is among you, not to think of *himself* more highly than he ought to think; but to think soberly, according as God hath dealt to every man the measure of faith. Romans 12:3

Availability: Having then gifts differing according to the grace that is given to us, whether prophecy, *let us prophesy* according to the proportion of faith; or ministry, *let us wait* on *our* ministering: or he that teacheth, on teaching; or he that exhorteth, on exhortation: he that giveth, *let him do it* with simplicity; he that ruleth, with diligence; he that sheweth mercy, with cheerfulness. Romans 12:6-8

Wisdom: If any of you lack wisdom, let him ask of God, that giveth to all *men* liberally, and upbraideth not; and it shall be given him. James 1:5

Neglect not the gift that is in thee, which was given thee by prophecy, with the laying on of the hands of the presbytery. 1 Timothy 4:1

REFLECTION

Take some time to reflect on today's devotion.

What are your thoughts on cultivating your gifts?

_____
_____
_____
_____
_____
_____

Do you believe you are working in your vocation according to your gifts?

_____
_____

Do a self-review. List your gifts and evaluate if your gifts are working in accordance with your vocation.

_____
_____
_____
_____
_____
_____
_____

If yes to the above, I encourage you to continue staying focused and in alignment with God to execute His ultimate plan.

If no, I encourage you to seek our heavenly Father for direction to enlighten your understanding of your gifts and enhance your vocation.

NO ONE LEFT BEHIND
Now that you have embraced the importance of cultivating your gift, how can you teach and encourage someone to do the same?

_____

_____

_____

_____

_____

_____

_____

_____

_____

_____

_____

_____

_____

_____

_____

_____

_____

Wisdom: If any of you lack wisdom, let him ask of God, that giveth to all *men* liberally, and upbraideth not; and it shall be given him.

James 1:5

JOURNAL YOUR DAY

_____

_____

_____

_____

_____

_____

_____

_____

_____

_____

_____

_____

_____

_____

_____

_____

_____

_____

_____

_____

_____

_____

_____

_____

Suzette A. Fox

_____
_____
_____
_____
_____
_____
_____
_____
_____
_____
_____
_____
_____
_____
_____
_____
_____
_____
_____
_____
_____
_____
_____
_____

And every wise hearted among you shall come, and make all that the Lord hath commanded. Exodus 35:10

Suzette A. Fox

27

WE OUGHT TO PROSPER

One might say that this title may be a bit obnoxious, but
when you are a child of God, a King's kid, we should never
think that we are not worthy of the prosperity that God has
for us. Our Father says in Psalm 24:1, "The earth *is* the
Lord's, and the fulness thereof; the world, and they that
dwell therein." He owns everything. For us to prosper, there
is a condition that we must meet and that is; OBEY!
Deuteronomy 11:26–27 says, "Behold, I set before you this
day blessing and a curse; a blessing, if ye obey the
commandments of the Lord your God, which I command
you this day." God told us in His word that He has provided
for us to prosper we can use that to shows us how God
prospers His people through our obedience. God made a
covenant with Abraham to be the father of many nations and
promised him that both he and his seed would be blessed in
abundance. Abraham was blessed with great riches. God
desires us to live in the plan He ordained for our life, and in
doing so, we will want for nothing. God does not desire for
us to lag behind Him or go before Him, but to walk in
alignment with Him. I am learning that as long as my spirit
is rich in Jesus, my physical body will be rich as well. It
goes hand in hand. God created us in His image and His
likeness and He is a prosperous God and takes pleasure in
our prosperity. He breathed life into our bodies (outer shell)

172

and we became a living soul. He also loves us so much that He allow us to choose. At the beginning of my adult life, not knowing better, I chose to please self, not knowing that I was submitting my soul to the devil to work on his behalf. But thank God for the blood. After being born again, I chose, through my free will, to allow my Creator to call all the shots in my life which had led me to experience and live a prosperous life. He alone is my boss and it's the best life ever! Jeremiah 29:11 NIV says, "'For I know the plans I have for you,' declares the Lord, 'plans to prosper you and not to harm you, plans to give you hope and a future.'"

Suzette A. Fox

MEDITATE:

The blessing of the LORD, it maketh rich, and he addeth no sorrow with it. Proverbs 10:22

Let them shout for joy, and be glad, that favour my righteous cause: yea, let them say continually, Let the Lord be magnified, which hath pleasure in the prosperity of his servant. Psalm 35:27

The LORD shall command the blessing upon thee in thy storehouses, and in all that thou settest thine hand unto; and he shall bless thee in the land which the LORD thy God giveth thee. Deuteronomy 28:8

He that is of a proud heart stirreth up strife: but he that putteth his trust in the LORD shall be made fat. Proverbs 28:25

REFLECTION

Take some time to reflect on today's devotion.

What are your thoughts on today's devotion?

_____

_____

_____

As you evaluate your life, do you believe you're living a prosperous life in God, naturally and spiritually?

_____

_____

_____

_____

_____

If yes, list the areas you've noticed you're prospering in? Are there any other areas in your spiritual and natural life that need to prosper?

_____

_____

_____

If no, list the areas in your life that need to prosper spiritually and naturally.

_____

_____

_____

_____

Assignment: Find scriptures pertaining to the areas in your spiritual and natural life that need to prosper. Take it to our heavenly Father in prayer until you see that change. Also meditate on Isaiah 62:6–7

NO ONE LEFT BEHIND
Now that you have embraced that God takes pleasure in seeing us prosper spiritually and naturally, how can you encourage others to embrace this godly principle?

_____

_____

_____

_____

_____

_____

_____

_____

_____

_____

_____

_____

_____

_____

For the Lord God *is* a sun and shield: the Lord will give grace and glory: no good *thing* will he withhold from them that walk uprightly.

Psalm 84:11

JOURNAL YOUR DAY

Suzette A. Fox

His soul shall dwell at ease; and his seed shall inherit the earth.
Psalm 25:13

28

SERVITUDE TO SERVANT

"*Let* nothing *be done* through strife or vainglory; but in lowliness of mind let each esteem other better than themselves" (Philippians 2:3). The word servitude is from an Old French word, *servitudo* and from Latin *servus* meaning *slave*. *Merriam-Webster's* defines servitude as "the state of being a slave." Romans 6:20 states, "For when ye were the [slave] of sin, ye were free from righteousness." This means before we came into the knowledge of Christ, we were in bondage to sin and yoked together or entangled with the many things that we engaged in. A slave does not have any say in regard to his or her wellbeing. Their hands are tied, they are not free to roam, and their every move is dictated by their owner. They become imprisoned, physically and mentally, thus less noticeable. Unfortunately, that's the state the enemy desires for us in our lives. Abandoning the life of servitude to become a servant, Jesus set a great example for us in Matthew 20:28: "Just as the Son of Man did not come to be served, but to serve, and to give his life as a ransom for many." Jesus came to become a servant to all. He left the throne of glory to suffer as a servant. *Merriam-Webster's Dictionary* defines servant as "one that serve others." Its origin is from the Old French word, *servir* (to serve), servant (person serving.) As a servant to mankind, Jesus took our sins, our diseases, our hurts and pain and it is this type of servant's heart that our Father delights for us to have. Psalm 34:4 says, "Delight thyself also in the Lord: and he shall give thee the desires of thine heart." To serve others is to delight in obedience and service with a humble heart and attitude. When we serve God, it brings great joy to Him in turn to serve us. We are all called to be servants (free, willing and available) not to be in servitude (bound, constrained by guilt or sin). A servant seeks the will of God as opposed to a person engaged in servitude who seeks their will. Mary and Martha are a great illustration of a servant's heart and a person operating in servitude. Mary was at the feet of Jesus (a servant), while Martha had her own agenda (servitude). Martha believed she had the right agenda, being busy while Jesus was in their presence, but at the same time she complained to Jesus of the stress she was under while Mary was serving at His feet "and heard his word" (Luke 10:39). These two actions had very different responses from Jesus. He said to Martha in verse 41, "thou art careful and troubled about many things" while He said Mary "hath chosen that good part" (verse 42). Wouldn't we all want Jesus to say that about us and the choices we make! Jesus made Martha understand that Mary was in right standing with Him, saying "that good part" shall "not be taken away from her." Even though Martha meant well preparing the home and meal for the guest, He would have loved for her to delight in His presence. Paraphrasing the story of Mary and Martha, Jesus is saying to us that as we move from a position of servitude to servant, delight in Him in obedience, serve Him and His people with a humble heart and attitude, and do not get busy of the cares of this world. When we serve His people, we serve Him. He desires that we always have a heart to serve so that we do not become distracted from the Great Commission.

MEDITATE:

If I then, *your* Lord and Master, have washed your feet; ye also ought to wash one another's feet. John 13:14

He saith to him again the second time, Simon, *son* of Jonas, lovest thou me? He saith unto him, Yea, Lord; thou knowest that I love thee. He saith unto him, Feed my sheep.
John 21:16

As we have therefore opportunity, let us do good unto all *men*, especially unto them who are of the household of faith.
Galatians 6:10

REFLECTION

Take some time to reflect on today's devotion.

What are your thoughts on today's devotion?

_____

_____

_____

As you search your heart, is there any area in your life where you are entangled in servitude?

_____

_____

_____

If yes, list those areas and find scriptures to bring before the Father in prayer.

_____

_____

_____

If no, I encourage you in your prayer time to ask our Father to reveal any area in your life that is entangled in servitude. Note: Some things may be hidden in your heart and may have a tendency to sneak up on you when you least expect it. Allow God to help you discover what may be hidden and deal with it.

Suzette A. Fox

As you search your heart, are there areas in your life where you desire to have more of a servant's heart?

_____

_____

_____

If yes, in your prayer time, seek our Father regarding those areas so that He can build you up to have a servant's heart.

If no, I encourage you to seek our Father in prayer allowing Him to show you areas in your life where you need to express a servant's heart.

NO ONE LEFT BEHIND
Now that you have embrace a better understanding of the difference between servitude and servant, how can you teach or encourage someone else to become a servant unto God?

_____

_____

_____

_____

_____

_____

_____

_____

Bear ye one another's burdens, and so fulfil the law of Christ.
Galatians 6:2

JOURNAL YOUR DAY

Suzette A. Fox

_____
_____
_____
_____
_____
_____
_____
_____
_____
_____
_____
_____
_____
_____
_____
_____
_____
_____
_____
_____
_____
_____
_____
_____
_____

For even the Son of man came not to be ministered unto, but to
minister, and to give his life a ransom for many.
Mark 10:45

Suzette A. Fox

29
SONSHIP

"For ye have not received the spirit of bondage again to fear; but ye have received the Spirit of adoption, whereby we cry, Abba, Father" (Romans 8:15). At one point in my walk with God, I had the misconception of Him being a taskmaster. I was taught what I "couldn't do" and to me, that meant that every time I messed up, it would be difficult for me to ask God for forgiveness. Those times that I would mess up became very trying for me as I always felt as though I needed to be perfect for God and that I had to do it in my own strength or else I would feel His wrath. As a result, I became engulfed in the spirit of rejection feeling jealous, offended, and insecure like I had to compete for God's love and approval. It was much like an orphan spirit. Someone with an orphan spirit is always looking for recognition from their father, be it their heavenly Father or natural father, and they also believe that by serving him they will earn His love. A person with an orphan spirit strives to exceed their capacity by chasing after soulish desires or after the riches of this world to please themselves and to receive accolades from others. An orphan spirit can also be very manipulative. Once I came into an understanding of the spirit of sonship, I was released from my entanglement with the orphan spirit. It was exciting to know that walking in sonship with God is basking in the presence, love and joy continually as my source of strength. Sonship will also bring us to a place where we are delighted to serve and celebrate our brothers, sisters and leaders' accomplishments without desiring any personal accolades. It also helps us to rely on God's direction to lead us to great opportunities without us trying to obtain our own success. When we see ourselves as sons of God or mature offspring, it helps us to be confident in who we are in Him. It enables us to serve others with an open heart to fulfill their destiny in Christ because we are operating with the heart of the Father. When sons and daughters know they have the affirmation of God in their souls, they can then rebuild other sons and daughters in Christ, and the cycle continues from generation to generation. One of the greatest gifts is for us to walk in the love of the Father, who "so loved the world, that he gave his only begotten Son, that whosoever believeth in him should not perish, but have everlasting life" (John 3:16). We have a great future with our Father by accepting the adoption of sonship and refusing to be an orphan. Our God is certainly a good, good, Father—the greatest of them all.

MEDITATE:

Having predestined us unto the adoption of children by Jesus Christ to himself, according to the good pleasure of his will. Ephesians 1:5

For though ye have ten thousand instructors in Christ, yet *have ye* not many fathers: for in Christ Jesus I have begotten you through the gospel.   1 Corinthians 4:15

And he humbled thee, and suffered thee to hunger, and fed thee with manna, which thou knewest not, neither did thy fathers know; that he might make thee know that man doth not live by bread only, but by every *word* that proceedeth out of the mouth of the Lord doth man live. Deuteronomy 8:3

For ye have not received the spirit of bondage again to fear; but ye have received the Spirit of adoption, whereby we cry, Abba, Father. Romans 8:15

REFLECTION

Take some time to reflect on today's devotion.

What are your thoughts on today's devotion?

_____

_____

_____

_____

Where do you stand today in your relationship with God? As a son or orphan?

_____

_____

_____

_____

As you search your heart, list why you feel you have an orphan relationship with God. Now take your concerns to our Father in prayer asking Him for the heart of a son of God.

_____

_____

_____

_____

_____

_____

As you search your heart, list why you feel you have a sonship relationship with God.

_____

_____

_____

_____

_____

_____

NO ONE LEFT BEHIND

Now that you have embraced the importance of sonship, how can you teach and encourage others to pursue that mature relationship with God as His son?

_____

_____

_____

_____

_____

_____

_____

_____

_____

_____

To redeem them that were under the law, that we might receive the adoption of sons. Galatians 4:5

JOURNAL YOUR DAY

Suzette A. Fox

_____
_____
_____
_____
_____
_____
_____
_____
_____
_____
_____
_____
_____
_____
_____
_____
_____
_____
_____
_____
_____
_____
_____

For ye have not received the spirit of bondage again to fear; but ye have received
the Spirit of adoption, whereby we cry, Abba, Father.
Romans 8:15

30

CULTIVATE YOUR HEART

"Keep thy heart with all diligence; for out of it are the issues of life" (Proverbs 4:23).

It is imperative that we position our hearts to receive the word of God daily and protect it with the breastplate of righteousness, as stated in Ephesians 6:14. "Stand therefore, having your loins girt about with truth, and having on the breastplate of righteousness." This scripture means that we are to stand strong in prayer and the word which will protect your heart from any wrong decisions or immoral actions. Apostle Paul used the gear that the Roman soldier wore as a comparison for us; as we are soldiers in Christ. He stated in Ephesians 6:12, "For we wrestle not against flesh and blood, but against principalities, against powers, against the rulers of the darkness of this world, against spiritual wickedness in high *places.*" He also told us how this gear will protect us through our spiritual warfare, as it did for the soldiers in the war. The breastplate protects the heart, which is a vital organ, spiritually and naturally. Naturally, the heart sends blood throughout our body. The blood provides our body with the oxygen and nutrients it needs. It also carries away waste. Our heart is similar to two pumps working as one. The right side of our heart receives blood from the body and pumps it to the lungs. The left side of the heart does the exact opposite: It receives blood from the lungs and pumps

Suzette A. Fox

it out to the body. Our spiritual heart pumps emotions and desires to our mind, body and soul, both positive and negative. To rid our spiritual hearts of the negative "waste," we have to condition ourselves to prayer, fasting, consecration and the word of God which will build the fruit of the spirit throughout our mind, body and soul. Guarding our hearts with the breastplate of righteousness will help us to make moral, ethical decisions and actions. Keeping our hearts pure, sanctified (set apart) is vital in staying in alignment with our Father.

MEDITATE:

My son, give me thine heart, and let thine eyes observe my ways.   Proverbs 23:26

Create in me a clean heart, O God; and renew a right spirit within me.   Psalm 51:10

My flesh and my heart faileth: *but* God *is* the strength of my heart, and my portion forever.   Psalm 73:26

Whose adorning let it not be that outward adorning of plaiting the hair, and of wearing of gold, or of putting on of apparel; But let it be the hidden man of the heart, in that which is not corruptible, even the ornament of a meek and quiet spirit. 1Peter 3:3-4

The heart is deceitful above all things, and desperately wicked: who can know it ?. I the LORD search the heart, I try the reins, even to give every man according to his ways, and according to the fruit of his doings. Jeremiah 17:9-10

REFLECTION

Take some time to reflect on today's devotion.

What are your thoughts on today's devotion?

_____

_____

_____

Take some time and search your heart. Is there anything hidden that you need to expose to God?

_____

_____

_____

_____

List those things and take it to our Father in prayer. Expose your heart to God because He desires to cultivate your heart.

_____

_____

_____

_____

_____

_____

_____

Keep a journal of your accomplishments as God cultivates your heart.

Suzette A. Fox

No one left behind

Now that you have embraced the importance of cultivating your heart, how can you help someone do the same?

_____

_____

_____

_____

_____

_____

_____

_____

_____

_____

_____

_____

_____

_____

_____

_____

_____

_____

_____

_____

_____

_____

And the peace of God, which passeth all understanding, shall keep your hearts and minds through Christ Jesus.
Philippians 4:7

JOURNAL YOUR DAY

Suzette A. Fox

_____
_____
_____
_____
_____
_____
_____
_____
_____
_____
_____
_____
_____
_____
_____
_____
_____
_____
_____
_____
_____
_____
_____
_____
_____

Trust in the Lord with all thine heart; and lean not unto thine own understanding.
Proverbs 3:5

Suzette A. Fox

31

PRAY ABOUT EVERYTHING

"Be careful for nothing; but in everything by prayer and supplication with thanksgiving let your requests be made known unto God. And the peace of God, which passeth all understanding, shall keep your hearts and minds through Christ Jesus" (Philippians 4:6–7). Therefore, our Father is saying to us there is no need to stress or be fearful about anything, a tactic the enemy uses to get us off focus on our assignments. God's desire for us is to come to Him as a little child about everything. Never think a situation is too big or too small to talk to our Father about. In a *HuffPost.com* blog, "The Important Role of Dad," the article defines one of the roles of a father as this: "Fathers are central to the emotional well-being of their children; they are capable caretakers and disciplinarians." This is the role of a natural father. Ultimately, the role of our heavenly Father is the same, but with a lot more added. Although our natural fathers may believe they know what is best for us, only our heavenly Father knows what's best as well as what's ahead of us. It's important and wise for us to consult with our Father to be sure our desire is His desire, our decisions line up with His will. This will prevent us from making irresponsible decisions. During the times that you may feel alone in prayer and may not have any words to utter, Jesus is there desiring to intercede through you. Don't become weary, continue to

200

press in "for we know not what we should pray for as we ought: but the Spirit itself maketh intercession for us with groanings which cannot be uttered" (Romans 8:26). Even when you are moaning and groaning deep within or sitting in His presence in silence, it is still prayer. Never think while you are in prayer that you have to do all the talking. God already knows what we need before we bring our petition to Him. Our petition to God should not take up our entire prayer time. Actually, we should be spending 20% of our time in petition and 80% of our time sitting in His presence listening to Him and agreeing with what He is saying to us with a "Yes, Lord." First John 5:14–15 says, "And this is the confidence that we have in him, that, if we ask any thing according to his will, he heareth us: and if we know that he hear us, whatsoever we ask, we know that we have the petitions that we desired of him." Once we agree with Him, we can rest assured that His "will be done" in our situations.

MEDITATE:

O thou that hearest prayer, unto thee shall all flesh come.
Psalm 65:2

Even them will I bring to my holy mountain, and make them joyful in my house of prayer: their burnt offerings and their sacrifices shall be accepted upon mine altar; for mine house *shall be* called an house of prayer for all people. Isaiah 56:7

And he said unto them, When ye pray, say, Our Father which art in heaven, Hallowed be thy name. Thy kingdom come. Thy will be done, as in heaven, so in earth. Luke 11:2

Rejoice evermore. Pray without ceasing. In every thing give thanks: for this is will of God in Christ Jesus concerning you. 1Thessaloninas 5:16-18

And this is the confidence that we have in him, that, if we ask any thing according to his will, he heareth us.
1 John 5:14

Source: *HuffPost.com*, Dr. Gail Gross, "The Important Role of Dad, *The Blog*, 6/12/2014, updated 8/12/2014, https://www.huffingtonpost.com/dr-gail-gross/the-important-role-of-dad_b_5489093.html.

Suzette A. Fox

REFLECTION

Take some time to reflect on today's devotion.

What are your thoughts on today's devotion?

_____

_____

How is your prayer life?

_____

_____

Do you experience any struggle in setting time to spend with God?

_____

_____

In your quest to set your schedule to spend valued time with God, be open to adjusting your schedule. Below, list your current schedule and place God at the beginning and at the end of each day. During the day, as you are thinking about the Father, automatically, you will utter prayers to Him. Beginning and ending your day with Him is sealing what He has already ordained for your day. Remember, be sure to thank Him for your accomplishments.

_____

_____

_____

_____

Suzette A. Fox

List your prayer requests and check them off as God answers them and gives you direction.

_____

_____

_____

I encourage you to develop a prayer journal. God will often speak during prayer time as it is a two-way communication. Be sure to make note of when He speaks to you and what He says in your journal. Be attentive and obey whatever His direction is for you.

NO ONE LEFT BEHIND
Now that you have embraced the importance of prayer, how can you teach and encourage someone in this area?

_____

_____

_____

_____

_____

_____

_____

_____

_____

Likewise the Spirit also helpeth our infirmities: for we know not what we should pray for as we ought: but the Spirit itself maketh intercession for us with groanings which cannot be uttered.
Romans 8:26

JOURNAL YOUR DAY

Suzette A. Fox

_____

_____

_____

_____

_____

_____

_____

_____

_____

_____

_____

_____

_____

_____

_____

_____

_____

_____

_____

_____

_____

_____

_____

And if we know that he hear us, whatsoever we ask, we know that we have the
petitions that we desired of him.
1 John 5:15

32

BE A PEACEMAKER

"Blessed are the peacemakers: for they shall be called the children of God" (Matthew 5:9). God is always ready to fight for us not in the natural, but in the spirit. He has always been very strategic, especially when fighting is "among the brethren", because the aggressor is also His child, and He must show love and mercy when disciplining. When our children get into a scuffle with their sibling, because we love both, we show mercy to the aggressor. God has called those of us walking in the light as the mature sibling to the younger, to set an example. And it doesn't matter if a person is in "the household of faith," or not. We, as a child of God, have a better understanding of who God is and His desires in spite of the discontent between us and our aggressor. No matter who the aggressor is, God will always look at us first to examine if we exercised the fruit of the Spirit. Galatians 5:22 and 23 says, "...the fruit of the Spirit is love, joy, peace, longsuffering, gentleness, goodness, faith, meekness, temperance: against such there is no law." When we allow the fruit of the Spirit to dictate our actions, it will bring Glory to God, and most importantly it's a witness to our aggressor as to what real love and mercy is. It's imperative for our eyes to be as high as an eagle's, being focused and ready to be the light and salt of this world. There is someone watching us at all times, waiting for the right moment to

Suzette A. Fox

examine our actions and response in difficult, uncommon, distasteful moments. Let's always choose to allow our light to shine and show the glory of our father.

MEDITATE:

Deceit *is* in the heart of them that imagine evil: but to the counsellors of peace *is* joy. Proverbs 12:20

Let us therefore follow after the things which make for peace, and things wherewith one may edify another. Romans 14:19

If it be possible, as much as lieth in you, live peaceably with all men. Romans 12:18

Pursue peace with all *men,* and the sanctification without which no one will see the Lord. Hebrews 12:14

Suzette A. Fox

REFLECTION

Take some time to reflect on today's devotion.

What are your thoughts on today's devotion?

_____

_____

_____

Do you believe you are a peacemaker?

_____

_____

_____

If no, list the areas in your life that you find bring confusion and discord. Take it to our heavenly Father in prayer with scriptures that pertain to who a peacemaker is. Do not give your prayer rest until you see a change.

_____

_____

_____

_____

_____

_____

_____

If yes, I encourage you to stay focused and continue to allow God's light to shine through you.

Suzette A. Fox

No one left behind

Now that you have embraced the importance of being a peacemaker, how can you teach and encourage someone else?

_____

_____

_____

_____

_____

_____

_____

_____

_____

_____

_____

_____

_____

_____

_____

_____

_____

_____

_____

Blessed *are* the peacemakers: for they shall be called the children of God.
Matthew 5:9

JOURNAL YOUR DAY

Suzette A. Fox

Depart from evil, and do good; seek peace, and pursue it..
Psalm 34:14

Suzette A. Fox

YOUR

ARMOUR

213

Suzette A. Fox

THE COMPLETE SUIT OF ARMOR

Large shield of faith

Helmet of salvation

Breastplate of righteousness

Sword of the spirit

Loins girded with truth

Feet shod with the equipment of the good news of peace

+ Every kind of prayer

214

For we wrestle not against flesh and blood, but against

principalities, against powers, against the rulers of the

darkness of this world, against spiritual wickedness in high
places.

Wherefore take unto you the whole armour of God, that ye
may be able to withstand in the evil day, and having done
all, to stand.

Stand therefore, having your loins girt about with truth, and
having on the breastplate of righteousness;

And your feet shod with the preparation of the gospel of
peace;

Above all, taking the shield of faith, wherewith ye shall be
able to quench all the fiery darts of the wicked.

And take the helmet of salvation, and the sword of the
Spirit, which is the word of God:

Praying always with all prayer and supplication in the
Spirit, and watching thereunto with all perseverance and
supplication for all saints.

Ephesians 6:12–18

33

WALK IN TRUTH

"Stand therefore, having your loins girt about with truth…" (Ephesians 6:14).

For us to stand in TRUTH, we have to know the word of God. I cannot stress the importance of knowing the word of God enough. If we do not know the word of God, we cannot win our battles that we fight in prayer or even when we have to stand in silence. The word of God is the TRUTH we can stand on. Jesus even had to stand on the truth of God's word when he was being tempted in Matthew 4:1–4, "Then was Jesus led up of the Spirit into the wilderness to be tempted of the devil. And when he had fasted forty days and forty nights, he was afterward an hungered. And when the tempter came to him, he said, If thou be the Son of God, command that these stones be made bread. But he answered and said, It is written, Man shall not live by bread alone, but by every word that proceedeth out of the mouth of God." Jesus had to gird His loins with the TRUTH; the word of God, therefore He was able to stand with all power and authority when the devil tried to tempt Him.

MEDITATE:

Jesus saith unto him, I am the way, the truth, and the life: no man cometh unto the Father, but by me. John 14:6

Pilate therefore said unto him, Art thou a king then? Jesus answered, Thou sayest that I am a king. To this end was I born, and for this cause came I into the world, that I should bear witness unto the truth. Everyone that is of the truth heareth my voice. John 18:37

He is the Rock, his work *is* perfect: for all his ways *are* judgment: a God of truth and without iniquity, just and right *is* he. Deuteronomy 32:4

My little children, let us not love in word, neither in tongue; but in deed and in truth. 1 John 3:18

If we say that we have fellowship with him, and walk in darkness, we lie, and do not the truth. 1 John 1:6

REFLECTION

Take some time to reflect on today's devotion.
Today, journal about what you have learned regarding
TRUTH; how it relates to who God is and any other
information you would like to meditate on later. This will
help you during your self-evaluation.

_____

_____

_____

_____

_____

_____

_____

_____

_____

_____

_____

_____

_____

_____

_____

_____

_____

_____

_____

_____

_____

Suzette A. Fox

_____

_____

_____

_____

_____

_____

_____

_____

_____

_____

NO ONE LEFT BEHIND

Now that you have embraced the importance in of walking in God's truth, how can you teach and encourage others?

_____

_____

_____

_____

_____

_____

_____

_____

_____

_____

Teach me thy way, O Lord; I will walk in thy truth: unite my heart to fear thy name.
Psalm 86:11

34

WALK IN RIGHTEOUSNESS

"...and having on the breastplate of righteousness" (Ephesians 6:14).

Being able to walk in righteousness depends on what is in our hearts. The Bible says, "For with the heart man believeth unto righteousness" (Romans 10:10). The breastplate was designed to cover the chest area or the heart specifically and Paul knew this when describing the Roman soldiers' gear and how it relates to spiritual battle which we talked about on Day 30's entry, "Cultivate Your Heart.". The breastplate symbolically protecting our heart with God's word is vital in our walk with God. Whatever we allow to penetrate into our heart, that's what will come out of our mouth for the Bible tells us, "for out of the abundance of the heart the mouth speaketh" (Matthew 12:34). We should always desire to build up and not tear down, as we are the light for the world and by doing so, we are allowing the world to see the Glory of God through us. We must search our hearts daily and allow God to show us those hidden things in our hearts that may be ungodly in nature letting Him purge us of them. In the end we only become better and not bitter.

Suzette A. Fox

MEDITATE:

I the Lord have called thee in righteousness, and will hold thine hand, and will keep thee, and give thee for a covenant of the people, for a light of the Gentiles. Isaiah 42:6

And Asa did that which was good and right in the eyes of the Lord his God. 2 Chronicles 14:2

There was a man in the land of Uz, whose name *was* Job; and that man was perfect and upright, and one that feared God, and eschewed evil. Job 1:1

And they were both righteous before God, walking in all the commandments and ordinances of the Lord blameless. Luke 1:6

He that followeth after righteousness and mercy findeth life, righteousness, and honor. Proverbs 21:21

REFLECTION

Take some time to reflect on today's devotion.
Today, journal about what you have learned regarding
RIGHTEOUSNESS and any other information you would
like to study and meditate later. This will help you during
your self-evaluation.

_____

_____

_____

_____

_____

_____

_____

_____

_____

_____

_____

_____

_____

_____

_____

_____

_____

_____

_____

_____

_____

_____

_____

_____

_____

_____

_____

_____

_____

NO ONE LEFT BEHIND

Now that you have embraced and have an understanding of God's **RIGHTEOUSNESS**, how can you teach and encourage others on what you have learnt?

_____

_____

_____

_____

_____

_____

_____

_____

_____

_____

And they were both righteous before God, walking in all the commandments and ordinances of the Lord blameless.

Luke 1:6

35

WALK IN PEACE

"And your feet shod with the preparation of the gospel of peace" (Ephesians 6:15)

"When a man's ways please the Lord, he maketh even his enemies to be at peace with him" (Psalm 16:7). When your enemies are at peace with you everybody wins because ultimately God's nature is shown through those that make peace. God loves when His children walk in peace, where we can reason together and allow His light to shine. He is not the author of confusion and He expects the same from His children. How would unbelievers know the love of God if we cannot reason together to work out our differences as brothers and sisters with those within the Body of Christ as well as with those who are outside of Christ? All eyes are always on us; those who confess they are children of God. We are always looked upon as the example of who God is; in us. God does not take sides, He loves all His children unconditionally, the just and the unjust. Never think God will look upon the unjust any different than the just in the event of a conflict. The thing He is most interested in is that the conflict's end result is peace. He will judge the peacemaker at a higher standard because we are to always represent Him as His children. Our hearts and minds must be in a pure place with God so that we can desire peace at all times. Allow God to search your heart and mind daily through prayer. Let His word permeate your heart by

Suzette A. Fox

renewing your mind daily and becoming the peacemaker
God desires of you.

MEDITATE:

Finally, brethren, farewell. Be perfect, be of good comfort,
be of one mind, live in peace; and the God of love and peace
shall be with you. 2 Corinthians 13:11

Those things, which ye have both learned, and received, and
heard, and seen in me, do: and the God of peace shall be
with you. Philippians 4:9

 And the very God of peace sanctify you wholly; and *I pray
God* your whole spirit and soul and body be preserved
blameless unto the coming of our Lord Jesus Christ.
1 Thessalonians 5:23

Blessed are the peacemakers: for they shall be called the
children of God. Matthew 5:9

And let the peace of God rule in your hearts, to the which
also ye are called in one body; and be ye thankful.
Colossians 3:15

REFLECTION

Take some time to reflect on today's devotion.
Today, journal about what you have learned regarding
walking in peace and any other information you would like
to meditate on. This will help you during your self-
evaluation.

_____

_____

_____

_____

_____

_____

_____

_____

_____

_____

_____

_____

_____

_____

_____

_____

_____

_____

_____

Suzette A. Fox

_____

_____

_____

_____

_____

_____

No one left behind

Now that you have embraced and have an understanding of **walking in God's PEACE**, how can you teach and encourage someone else?

_____

_____

_____

_____

_____

_____

_____

_____

_____

_____

_____

Those things, which ye have both learned, and received, and heard, and seen in me, do: and the God of peace shall be with you.
Philippians 4:9

36

WALK IN FAITH

"Above all, taking the shield of faith, wherewith ye shall be able to quench all the fiery darts of the wicked" (Ephesians 6:16)

When we walk in faith, we know who God is and that He is one with His word. When we obey God's word we shield ourselves of any fiery darts from the adversary which equals walking in faith. Faith is also "the substance of things hoped for, the evidence of things not seen" (Hebrew 11:1). Therefore, faith is stepping out on what the natural eyes cannot see. Abraham, one of the greatest men in the Bible, depicted great faith in Genesis 22. To have such faith meant that Abraham spent a lot of time with God. He knew His heartbeat, what moved God, and what God would and would not do. Abraham trusted God wholeheartedly. God takes pleasure in us giving up our control to love, depend, consult and wait on Him in all that we do. He desires to unconditionally love and serve us as we serve Him wholeheartedly. If you feel your faith is a bit low, pray daily asking God to increase your faith. Don't allow your trials to break you down but build you up to divine faith. The just shall live by faith and as we lean and depend on God, our walk in faith will show who God is in our lives.

MEDITATE:

For therein is the righteousness of God revealed from faith to faith: as it is written, The just shall live by faith. Romans 1:17

And the apostles said unto the Lord, Increase our faith. And the Lord said, If ye had faith as a grain of mustard seed, ye might say unto this sycamine tree, Be thou plucked up by the root, and be thou planted in the sea; and it should obey you. Luke 17:5–6

So then faith cometh by hearing, and hearing by the word of God. Romans 10:17

Therefore I say unto you, What things soever ye desire, when ye pray, believe that ye receive them, and ye shall have them. Mark 11:24

REFLECTION

Take some time to reflect on today's devotion.
Today, journal about what you have learned regarding
walking in faith and any other information you would like
to study and meditate. This will help you during your self-
evaluation.

_____

_____

_____

_____

_____

_____

_____

_____

_____

_____

_____

_____

_____

_____

_____

_____

_____

_____

_____

_____

_____

_____

_____

_____

_____

_____

_____

_____

_____

No one left behind

Now that you have embraced and understand what is involved with **walking in FAITH**, how can you teach and encourage someone else?

_____

_____

_____

_____

_____

_____

_____

_____

_____

_____

_____

_____

_____

_____

So then faith cometh by hearing, and hearing by the word of God.

Romans 10:17

37

WALK IN SALVATION

" And take the helmet of salvation…" (Ephesians 6:17).

Salvation is deliverance from the power and penalty of sin. "For by grace are ye saved through faith; and that not of yourselves: it is the gift of God: Not of works, lest any man should boast" (Ephesians 2:8–9). Paul used the helmet of salvation in Ephesians, chapter 6, which protects our head where our thoughts and mind can be attacked during spiritual battles. Our adversary takes pleasure in tormenting our mind when we are confronted with any situation. When we come to the knowledge of who we are in God and know that our salvation or being saved from sin is a gift from God, we can then walk in victory winning the battle of the mind and proudly wear our helmet of salvation to conquer all adversity from our adversary. However, when we accept our gift of salvation by repenting and being born again of the water and the Spirit (Acts 2:38) we must continue to captivate our mind with the word of God and prayer, so that we will not be deceived by our adversary. With the helmet of salvation in place protecting our head, face and the back of our neck, we can now focus on being like God and aligning ourselves for the promise.

MEDITATE:

The Lord *is* my light and my salvation; whom shall I fear? the Lord *is* the strength of my life; of whom shall I be afraid?   Psalm 27:1

But the salvation of the righteous *is* of the Lord: *he is* their strength in the time of trouble.   Psalm 37:39

He only *is* my rock and my salvation; *he is* my defence; I shall not be greatly moved.   Psalm 62:2

Truly my soul waiteth upon God for him cometh my salvation. Psalm 62:1

And it shall come to pass, that whosoever shall call on the name of the Lord shall be saved. Acts 2:21

Suzette A. Fox

REFLECTION

Take some time to reflect on today's devotion.
Today, journal about what you have learned regarding
walking in salvation and any other information you would
study and meditate. This will help you during your self-
evaluation.

_____

_____

_____

_____

_____

_____

_____

_____

_____

_____

_____

_____

_____

_____

_____

_____

_____

_____

_____

_____

_____

_____

_____

_____

_____

_____

_____

NO ONE LEFT BEHIND

Now that you have embraced and understand **walking in salvation**, how can you teach and encourage others?

_____

_____

_____

_____

_____

_____

_____

_____

_____

_____

_____

_____

He only *is* my rock and my salvation; *he is* my defence; I shall not be greatly moved.   Psalm 62:2

38

WALK IN THE WORD

"…and the sword of the Spirit, which is the word of God" (Ephesians 6:17).

"Thy word *is* a lamp unto my feet, and a light unto my path" (Psalm 119:105). Every verse in Psalm 119 speaks of God's word or His law so we can see from these 176 reminders in this one Psalm alone how important it is to know and walk in the word. When you walk in the word of God, His word will keep us through those tough times. Hiding the word of God in your heart will also protect you from being deceived by our adversary. Just as the enemy tried to tempt Jesus, he will try to do the same to us. As we read in Matthew 4:1–11, Jesus responded to the devil with the word of God, but the devil did not let up just because Jesus used God's word. From Jesus' first response of "no," we see that the devil kept pursuing to tempt Him. Each time he tried to tempt Jesus, Jesus responded with God's word with boldness and confidence. This is a great example for us to never retreat when tempted but fight with the word of God until the enemy retreats. God's word carries all of the power and authority we need to fight off our adversary. Standing on the word of God will keep us from compromising because it will give us the strength to stand firm and stand strong, never to wither in a storm. The word is our sure foundation.

MEDITATE:

Wherewithal shall a young man cleanse his way? by taking heed *thereto* according to thy word. Psalm 119:9

This *is* my comfort in my affliction: for thy word hath quickened me. Psalm 119:50

He sendeth forth his commandment *upon* earth: his word runneth very swiftly. Psalm 147:15

Now the parable is this: The seed is the word of God.
Luke 8:11

REFLECTION

Take some time to reflect on today's devotion.
Today, journal about what you have learned regarding
walking in the word and any other information you would
like to study and meditate on. This will help you during your
self-evaluation.

_____
_____
_____
_____
_____
_____
_____
_____
_____
_____
_____
_____
_____
_____
_____
_____
_____
_____
_____
_____

_____
_____
_____
_____
_____
_____
_____

No one left behind

Now that you have embraced and understand the purpose of **walking in the word,** how can you teach and encourage someone else?

_____
_____
_____
_____
_____
_____
_____
_____
_____
_____

Now the parable is this: The seed is the word of God.

Luke 8:11

39

WALK IN YOUR PURPOSE

What is my purpose? This question is asked by many and at times, it goes unanswered. God created us all with a purpose and He desires for us to walk in it to fulfill His plan. In John 4:34, the Bible says, "Jesus saith unto them, My meat is to do the will of Him that sent me, and to finish his work." Jesus knew the importance of finishing the work that our Father has sent us to do. To do that, we must seek God's face in prayer and wait for His response. Too many times we have created our own purpose and were deceived into believing that we were living in God's purpose. We are all unique and wonderfully made with gifts and callings that God has placed in us and that only we can accomplish with Him, so it's imperative that we walk in our purpose and not someone else's.

MEDITATE:

But seek ye first the kingdom of God, and his righteousness; and all these things shall be added unto you. Matthew 6:33

I have glorified thee on the earth: I have finished the work which thou gavest me to do. John 17:4

There are many devices in a man's heart; nevertheless the counsel of the Lord, that shall stand. Proverbs 19:21

For the LORD of hosts, has planned, and who can frustrate it? And as for His stretched-out hand, who can turn it back? Isaiah 14:27

He made known to us the mystery of His will, according to His kind intention which He purposed in Him. Ephesians 1:9

REFLECTION

Take some time to reflect on today's devotion.
Today, journal about what you have learned regarding
walking in your purpose and any other information you
would like to study and meditate on. This will help you
during your self-evaluation.

_____

_____

_____

_____

_____

_____

_____

_____

_____

_____

_____

_____

_____

_____

_____

_____

_____

_____

_____

_____

_____

_____

_____

_____

_____

_____

No One Left Behind

Now that you have embraced and understand the purpose in **walking in your purpose**, how can you help someone else?

_____

_____

_____

_____

_____

_____

_____

_____

_____

_____

_____

_____

I have glorified thee on the earth: I have finished the work which thou gavest me to do.   John 17:4

40

GOD HAS A PLAN FOR YOU

"For I know the thoughts that I think toward you, saith the Lord, thoughts of peace, and not of evil, to give you an expected end" (Jeremiah 29:11). God's ultimate plan is to lead, direct and prosper us in all that we do. To fulfill our purpose on earth, we have to align our heart to God's heart, hear directly from Him and trust Him. No longer can we desire our plan. We have to put away our soulish desires and pursue His desires. I prefer to walk blindfolded in God's plan than to walk blindfolded in my plan.

MEDITATE:

For this *is* good and acceptable in the sight of God our Saviour; Who will have all men to be saved, and to come unto the knowledge of the truth. 1 Timothy 2:3–4

In everything give thanks: for this is the will of God in Christ Jesus concerning you. 1 Thessalonians 5:18

If any of you lack wisdom, let him ask of God, that giveth to all *men* liberally, and upbraideth not; and it shall be given him. James 1:5

A man's heart deviseth his way: but the Lord directeth his steps. Proverbs 16:9

REFLECTION

Take some time to reflect on today's devotion.
Today, journal about what you have learned regarding
walking in God's plan and any other information you
would like to study and meditate. This will help you during
your self-evaluation.

_____

_____

_____

_____

_____

_____

_____

_____

_____

_____

_____

_____

_____

_____

_____

_____

_____

_____

_____

_____

_____

_____

_____

_____

_____

_____

_____

_____

_____

No One Left Behind

Now that you have embraced and understand how important is to walk in God's plan, how can you teach and encourage someone else?

_____

_____

_____

_____

_____

_____

_____

_____

_____

For I know the thoughts that I think toward you, saith the Lord, thoughts of peace, and not of evil, to give you an expected end.

Jeremiah 29:11

PRAYER

Abba, Father, I thank you for sustaining me for these forty days of basking in you, coming to know who I am in you, understanding my purpose and to now continue in your will with your armour. Father, I ask that you keep my mind in perfect peace, never allowing the enemy to get the best of me because of all that I have learned from these forty days with you, and all that you have purged out of me and poured into me to be the child of God that you called me to be. I pray that I will never get off focus even in dry times and that I will keep my eyes on you, in your word, pursuing you to bask in your presence. Father, my heart's desire is to always pursue you reminding you of your word for my life day and night. Father, I desire to do all that you have planned for my life and to help those that you have assigned to me, to rebuild and to pour into them for your glory and for your

purpose. IN JESUS NAME

Suzette A. Fox

WORD OF ENCOURAGEMENT

Now that you have completed your forty days of fasting, prayer and consecration, I admonish you to carry what you have learned close to your heart. God has a great plan for your life, and the only way you will be able to see the plan come into fruition is to stay in alignment with Him even when it becomes difficult. Press your way, draw from His word, stay in a place of worship and stay connected to those that will help pour into you God's truth. From this day forward, it will not be easy, now that you have surrendered your all to God because the enemy will come to make you to second guess what you are doing. However, I admonish you to be strong and courageous because as long as your mind is made up, you will draw the strength to fight the good fight of faith. Child of God, go forth and let God use you for such a time as this. May God bless all that you do for His glory

ABOUT THE AUTHOR

Suzette Fox was born on April 21, on the beautiful island of Trinidad and Tobago. Suzette migrated to the United States at the age of 17 and she is the eldest of six siblings. She is married with three children, she also raised two additional children and inherited three grandchildren, whom she loves dearly. Suzette graduated from Carapichaima Senior Comprehensive School of Trinidad and Tobago, class of 1991, and she also attended Mercer County Community College in West Windsor, New Jersey, for two years pursuing her degree in business. She also completed several certificates for use in the healthcare industry.

In her local church, Suzette has been an active member of several ministries including outreach, intercession and intercessory prayer, usher, transportation, housekeeping, and she has also assisted in church planting. Suzette always had a passion to help build up others and she is now pursuing becoming a licensed Clinical Chaplain and a Pastoral Counselor.

Suzette A. Fox

After being called away from her job in 2016, God has been preparing Suzette for full-time ministry. She is also preparing to go into business as the owner of Lifetime Investments. In addition, Suzette is an aspiring author. Her business, Lifetime Investments, will be focused on the whole person through investing in a person's life, both spiritually and naturally. Suzette has desired this assignment for many years and believes that as she answers the call to this mission, she is finally walking in her purpose towards her destiny.

LET'S STAY CONNECTED

Thank you for purchasing Suzette Fox's first of many books. She prays that this book was and will continue to be a blessing to you as it was a blessing to her, allowing God to pour in and out of her onto these pages. Suzette would love to hear from you. Feel free to submit your reviews on Amazon, or on her website. Should you desire Suzette Fox to be a guest speaker at your event, please contact her via her website. You can also follow her on social media for upcoming events, updates on any new book projects and for lots of fun giveaways.

Website: www.suzetteafox.org

Email: SuzetteAFox@gmail.com

Facebook: /SuzetteAFox

Instagram: @SuzetteAFox

Twitter: @SuzetteAfox